Coleen's
REAL STYLE

Coleen Rooney

HarperCollins*Publishers*

To my mum and dad. Thanks for putting up with me for all these years and coping with my love of clothes! I appreciate everything you have done for me and for going out of your way to give me all you can (the expensive Christmas coats, ha ha). And mum, thanks for introducing me to all the girly things in life.

To my Wayne. Thanks for all your support in everything I do. I love you. And yes, I do need all those bags and shoes … because I love them!

HarperCollins*Publishers*
77–85 Fulham Palace Road,
Hammersmith, London W6 8JB
www.harpercollins.co.uk

First published by HarperCollins*Publishers* 2008

1

Photography © David Venni
Editor: Caragh McKay
Consultant Stylist: Jackie Dixon

A catalogue record of this book is available from the British Library

ISBN-13   978-0-00-723619-0
ISBN-10   0-00-723619-0

Printed and bound in Italy
L.E.G.O. SpA

Mixed Sources
Product group from well-managed forests and other controlled sources
www.fsc.org Cert no. SW-COC-1806
© 1996 Forest Stewardship Council
FSC

FSC is a non-profit international organisation established to promote the responsible management of the world's forests. Products carrying the FSC label are independently certified to assure consumers that they come from forests that are managed to meet the social, economic and ecological needs of present and future generations.

Find out more about HarperCollins and the environment at
www.harpercollins.co.uk/green

While every effort has been made to provide credits for the clothing and accessories that appear in the book, the publishers would like to apologize for any errors or omissions and will be pleased to amend credits accordingly in any future edition of this book.

ENDPAPERS Dress, Temperley London; shoes, Jimmy Choo.
TITLE PAGE Dress, Couture Couture.
RIGHT Shoes, Christian Louboutin.

contents

what is real style?

What Is Real Style?

Experimenting and finding the styles that best suit your look.

Everyone who knows me knows that I love fashion, and by that I don't mean going out and hitting the shops and spending until I drop, no matter what the papers say. It's just that, like most girls I know, I simply enjoy clothes and love trying out new looks and styles. I've never really been into full-on fashion-y looks, though. Don't get me wrong, I love seeing all the new styles from the catwalks every summer and winter and trying some of them out, but at the end of the day I'm a real girl with a real shape. And that means that no matter how much I love all the things I see, there are plenty of styles that are just never, ever going to do it for me.

I love all the catwalk looks, but I'm a real girl with a real shape.

And that's where my Real Style guide comes in. It's not about telling you the latest designer clothes to buy or just pointing out what's in fashion now, it's about me sharing my experiences with you and showing you some great ways to help you look and feel your best. Because whether you like to dress up in the latest designer gear, or love high street faves like Topshop (and who doesn't?), to me, real style does not come from copying someone else's look or wearing a designer name from top to toe. At the end of the day, whatever you decide to wear the only name that should be all over your look is yours.

 LEFT Photograph © WireImage/Getty Images
 ABOVE Handbag, La Redoute

My top five

So let's get started: I think the best way to do this is to take you through my idea of what makes a great, easy-to-wear set of clothes and styles – or 'capsule wardrobe'. That's what this section of the book is all about. I'll come back to certain things in the following chapters, like tops and bottoms and dresses. Oh, and don't worry, I've dedicated a whole chapter to jeans, so we'll look at these in loads more detail later on.

But don't flick through to that bit just yet; we're going to back to basics first. This is how I do it: when I'm deciding what to wear, I ask myself *five* key questions when I look at my outfit in the mirror:

Style Tip

It's OK if a shaped jacket won't button around the waist but fits well at the shoulders. Buttoned-up can look too office-like anyway, so just wear it loose – the nipped-in cut of it will still highlight one of your best bits – your waist.

1 Is this the right size?

Whether you're a real boho-chic girl or love the sexy, fitted look, the bottom line is that whatever you wear, you want to feel comfortable. You don't want to look too comfortable, though – I love chilling out and pottering about the house in my Juicy trackies, but they really won't do for a big night out! No, what I mean is making sure that your clothes fit well, because this is really the first step to not just looking good but feeling good too.

Think of the times you've gone out wearing something that is too tight, only to spend the whole time trying to hold your tummy in and looking like you're sucking a lemon. Or, if you feel your skirt is too short, you end up spending the evening pulling the hem, trying to wriggle it down all the time.

So it really is best to always wear clothes that fit well; that are the right size and in shapes that make the most of your figure – day and night. After all, why would you want to let anything get in the way of shopping, having fun or dancing the night away?

Top, Yves Saint Laurent; skirt, Joseph.

2 Which are my best bits?

It really helps to get to grips with the shape of your body, as this will give you a head start in finding the basic clothes shapes that suit you. Most of us go up and down in weight a bit but, generally, whether we are having a 'fat' or a 'thin' day, our basic shape stays the same. Mine is classic British pear: I've got quite a round bum (Wayne's really cheeky and says it looks big when I wear my Juicy tracksuits). I don't mind my shape and it's not likely to change that much, so I always dress to make the most of it.

Jacket, French Connection; shoes, George at Asda; belt, Mexx.

I think my best bit is my waist, though, as it's quite petite. This gives my body good proportion and balances out my shape, so I mostly go for clothes that highlight it. Big belts are brilliant for this. Also, as you can see, I'm definitely not the tall, leggy type, so I always have to take my height – and short legs – into consideration when buying new clothes. (Now you know why I love my heels.)

I have to be honest, though, understanding how your own body shape fits with the styles you like is one of the hardest things to get right, and it's taken me ages to figure it out. But when you have you'll realize that getting the balance right makes a huge difference. Because I know what shape I am, it makes it so much easier to pick styles that fit. So I always love things that come in at the waist and that highlight my shoulders – like a Grecian-style dress, or skinny jeans and a floaty top. And, of course, my Christian Louboutin stilettoes.

Real Style Note

- If you're having a 'fat' day, wear clothes that are looser but not too baggy, as you don't want to look shapeless. Again, it's about highlighting your good bits.

- Jeans can also feel a bit pinchy in places, so if you're not feeling your best, go for an outfit that flows a bit more, like a nice silky shirt and skirt, or softer, tailored jeans (7 For All Mankind do good ones).

- Wear something that you always feel good in, even if it is a bit dressy. A little extra glamour can go a long, long way.

3 Does this style really suit me?

Most of the time, you slip on a new top with a pair of your favourite jeans and you feel great. But sometimes, I have to admit, it's not that easy. You look in the mirror and think 'hmm?' before realizing that sometimes the look that really works for your mate, or that looked good on the girl in the shop, doesn't quite have the same effect on you. I know the feeling. I mean, I love to look good, but, like most fashion-lovers, I've had my fair share of fashion disasters. And there are sure to be many more 'What was I thinking?' moments to come…

Sometimes, if you take a chance, you can be really surprised at the results.

But of course we can't all be perfect, and that's just fine, because I really don't think that's what looking good is all about. In fact, over the past few years, I've come to the conclusion that none of us, no matter how fashionable or famous, ever gets it 100 per cent right.

ABOVE Top and skirt, Balenciaga. Photograph © Nils Jorgensen/Rex Features.

The only way I can work out what suits me best is by trying on the things I like. I've even taught myself to stop walking past things that I don't think are my style as I've realized that, sometimes, if you take a chance, you can be really surprised at the results. One of my favourite ever outfits was a little Balenciaga miniskirt and silk blouse that I wore to the Closer Young Heroes 2006 awards. I have never been a lover of minis, as I didn't think they would flatter my legs, but Justine at Cricket, my favourite designer boutique, encouraged me to try this one out. I think it was because the skirt flared out a little at the bottom, in an A-line shape, that it felt a bit different. I decided to wear it with opaque black tights. My legs didn't feel too big after all. That was a real result. But I really am comfortable with the fact that I won't always get it right. I think it would take all the fun out of fashion for me if I did.

Real Style Note

- Challenging your usual style can be a real confidence-booster and can make you look at your body shape in a more positive, way.

- If you live in jeans and T-shirts, the Boho, or 'new hippy' look might be a good one for you. Try wearing jeans and 1970s-style blouses with floaty sleeves, and add some necklaces and pendants. (Freedom at Topshop and Accessorize are brilliant for jewellery with a little more edge.)

- If you think that certain shapes are not your thing, just try loads of different brands on — from high-street styles to more expensive looks. It takes some effort, but keep searching and trying stuff on, you will be surprised at what you find.

4 Is it time to get a second opinion?

We all have these moments when we realize that something we've just bought is not quite right or that it doesn't really look the way you saw it in your head. So, if no matter how many times you look in the mirror you just don't feel sure about it, it's time to get a second opinion.

This can be a little bit tricky, because if you ask your close friends if something that you're not sure of looks good on you, the chances are that they might not want to hurt your feelings by saying what they really think. At this point I call in the expert: my mum. I'll often get ready to go out at my mum's in Liverpool, as I go out a lot there with my mates. My mum's really good at telling me if something's not quite right, and I trust her opinion. She'll just say 'not sure' if she doesn't think it looks good.

Real Style Note

- Remember that if you ask for an opinion you might not get the response you had hoped for. So try to take it on the chin and don't take it out on the person you asked.

- If someone asks for your opinion, it's always better to be honest, but at the same time to be a little gentle with the truth.

- Be as encouraging as you can and make any suggestions based on that person's usual style.

RIGHT Dress, Lanvin.

I don't always agree with what they say, though, so I'll maybe just go with my first choice anyway. Some of my mates will ask their big sisters for help. Wouldn't it be great if we could all just hit the shops and bring back one of those?

Style Tip

It's best not to wear skirts too short – for obvious reasons – but if you like wearing minis, then styles that sit just above the knees are a good bet. Try wearing them with thick, black tights or leggings in winter. The bare-leg look is not one that many people can carry off. Especially in cold weather! But, if you have the legs for minis, why not!

5 How should I do my hair and make-up?

Getting your hair and make-up right is another one of those things that takes years to work out. I've never really been one for much make-up: I usually just put gloss on my lips and often I don't even bother with mascara. But while that suits me fine during the day, I always put a little more thought into how I look for going out at night.

I loved the way Kate Moss had a star painted in gold eyeshadow across one eye on the night of her 34th birthday party. But that's Kate's real style and it just wouldn't be me to go for something like that. So, while I would never suggest that you hit the eyeshadow palette with a paintbrush, there's no doubt that if you're glamming up for a night, just keeping it natural can make you look too washed out. The way I do it is simply to make my daytime look a little stronger. So, I'll put on some black mascara, brush on some bronzer and maybe wear a darker lip gloss.

Of course, like most girls, I could go on forever about my hair. But my general rule is to pull it into a ponytail for day, and to wear it soft and loose or sleek and straight at night. If you've got short hair, add some glossing product and make it a little sleeker – spiky hairdos can look a little fierce. If your hair's curly, add some moisturizing anti-frizz spray for healthy-looking locks and tease your curls out a little at night – and if it's short, pull and lift the waves back from your face. But don't be afraid to experiment: I did just that when I went to Victoria and David Beckham's Full Length and Fabulous party in 2006, and my hairdresser pulled my hair up into a top bun. I'm not sure if I'd go for that look again but, like Kate Moss, I had fun trying it out.

I like to stick to a natural make-up look and soft, neutral colours.

❀ LEFT Top, Hennes; ring, vintage.

❀ Brushes, The Body Shop.

Shaping up:

Styles to suit your body shape.

Over the past couple of years, I've been lucky to get loads of advice from the style professionals I've met on photo shoots (and I'm passing on lots of their tips, so 'thanks' to all of you). But the main reason I wanted to do my Real Style guide was to share my love of fashion with you, and to let you know how I've worked out the best ways of making the most of my own style.

I think real style is about constantly developing and changing your ideas.

Like most normal girls, it took me a while to get the confidence to develop my own tastes in clothes. And I've mostly done that just by trusting what I see in the mirror. I've still got lots to learn, but then to me that's what real style is all about: mine is constantly developing and we all change our ideas about what we like as we get older. There are some things, though, that I would never change: having the confidence to make your own choices, feeling good about the way you look, and, most of all, just being true to yourself.

LEFT Top, DKNY; skirt, DKNY.

Which shape are you?

SUPER LADYLIKE Then you'll tend to have a curvy bust and bum or thighs, and a nice, neat waist.

Styles to suit your shape Try simple, lower-cut necklines: anything too fussy can make you look square. Longer-length tops pulled in with a big wide belt will make your body look longer (I love tan-coloured leather ones as they go with everything. Try Reiss for a selection); nipped-in jackets show off the waist, shoulders and all your nice curvy bits to their best advantage. Try wearing skinny jeans with a longer floaty top to cover the bottom – this is one of my favourite looks for going out. Make sure that your trousers are not too short, as this can make you look a little square or stocky; A-line, just-below-the-knee skirts can really balance your shape out; and pencil skirts look fab worn with that lovely big belt.

GORGEOUSLY CURVY Then you might have more of a tummy, and nice, shapely legs, too.

Styles to suit your shape Try pretty necklines detailed with pleating, bows or ruching, as they will draw attention away from your middle – I think See by Chloé and Topshop do really good tops and T-shirts like this. Or try V-necks, as these will highlight your bust more and give the impression of narrowing the top of your body. Hipster belts will make the best of slim hips, and nipped-in jackets are also good for making you appear to have more of a waist. I would also try slim-cut trousers or jeans.

Dress, Marks & Spencer.

TALL AND LEGGY Your lovely, slim frame means you'll look really good in simple outfits like jeans and a T-shirt.

Styles to suit your shape Try plain tops in fresh colours such as white or powdery blue and coral pink, and dress them up with long necklaces and accessories. I think Elle Macpherson carries this style off so well. She sometimes even does her casual look when you see pictures of her on evenings out and she still looks fantastic. Another good idea is plain shirts – I got a blue-and-white striped one from the Kate Moss Topshop range, which looks really smart during the day. Bigger blouse styles can also look great when going out. Slim trousers or 'boyfriend' styles (Gap is brilliant for these) will look really stylish. And you'll be able to wear long, ruffle skirts and full-length maxi dresses. That's a look I love for summer.

Real Style Quiz

Now it's time to check your Real Style factor.
If you agree with any the following, tick the boxes next to them:

☐ I love choosing new clothes

☐ I love shopping with my mates

☐ I love getting dressed up

☐ I love looking good

☐ I love feeling good

If you answered YES to all of the above, you're totally in tune with your Real Style.

If you answered YES to three of the above, you might need a little fine-tuning.

If you answered NO to more than three of the above, you've got a Real Style journey ahead.

dresses

Dresses

From pretty prom styles to everyday shirt dresses, here's my guide to the key styles.

I think dresses are more fashionable now than they have ever been; and for a girly girl like me, this is great news, as I absolutely love wearing dresses.

For anyone who thinks that dresses are not their thing, now, with so many looks to choose from, you can be sure to find one that will make you look and feel gorgeous.

I find dresses so easy to wear; a one-stop route to looking good – I just pull one on, add a pair of earrings or a belt, and I'm ready to go. However, some people see dresses as a bit of a frumpy choice, or a fashion 'no-no'.

Dresses are a one-stop route to looking good.
I just pull one on and I'm ready to go.

The way to prevent a fuddy-duddy look, though, is to just go for a style that doesn't look too much like something your nan might wear. (But having said that, my nan always looks great.) No, what I mean is, be careful not to go for something that might make you look old before your time. Again, the best trick of all is picking clothes to suit your body shape. Once you've got that sorted, there'll be no stopping your girly side taking over.

The thing I love most about wearing dresses is the fact that they always look so pretty and feminine; and that is exactly how I feel when I wear one. All the big designers create loads of lovely new dresses for their summer and winter collections these days and there's always something for everyone and every occasion – from draped, Grecian styles to crisp, cotton shifts and show-stopping diva numbers.

So this chapter is about revealing some of the best dress looks of the moment – from day dresses to party dresses, including those classic shapes to suit any style. Here I'm going to help you discover which dresses might be best for you; some looks you might want to try, and some great little styling tips that I've picked up along the way.

✿ PREVIOUS PAGE Dress, Warehouse; shoes, Moschino.

✿ LEFT Dress, Balenciaga. Photograph © Paul Ellis/AFP/Getty Images.

✿ ABOVE Dress, Boohoo.com.

Five classic dress styles

Whether you like feeling girly as can be or prefer to keep things nice and simple, there's a dress to suit your shape. Here are five of my favourite styles:

THE PROM
Perfect for real girly girls

All the glossies talk about how fashion has become ultra-feminine over the past few years, and looking at the prom styles by the likes of Chanel, Luella and Beyond Retro, I can see what they mean. Maybe it has something to do with the fact that *Sex and the City's* Carrie pulls off the look so well. I just love when Carrie steps out of the door of her New York apartment in a big-skirted vintage dress, with her coat or jacket hanging casually over her shoulders. There's a real edginess to this look.

Getting the fit right

Prom dresses are all about the waist, so really, as long as the middle part of your dress is clasped in with a big belt or structured band, it's a look that will suit most figures. The reason that prom dresses are so girly is that the shape focuses on all the feminine parts of our bodies: the waist, neck, shoulders and lower legs. It's a particularly good look for curvy shapes. If you are not too confident about your upper arms, do what I do and use a scarf as a pretty wrap across your shoulders.

RIGHT Dress, Beyond Retro.

Fitting the prom dress into your style

The prom dress look can be a little over the top, so if you don't want to go too far with it, I'd choose a full-ish skirt that doesn't have any bouncy layers of netting, and wear a little cardi on top. You can create a more nipped-in look at the waist with a big, wide belt, and definitely wear heels – well, I always do – as you need the extra lift to balance out the volume of the skirt. If you keep your legs bare (with a hint of colour), it looks more elegant, but matt tights will do for winter. If you want to accessorize, I'd pick something that's not too fussy, as the dress is a statement in itself. Go for classic jewellery: drop earrings will make your neck look longer, especially if you don't wear a necklace. And ask your nan if you can have a good rummage through her jewellery box.

Prom dresses are so girly because they are such a feminine shape.

THE SHIFT

Perfect for keeping it simple

I find the straight-up-and-down style of shift dresses really easy to wear, and there are so many variations around that you can create lots of different looks. Lindsay Lohan looks brilliant in those Sixties-style mini-shifts, and I bought a fantastic patterned one by Milly, which I got from Cricket (but it's also stocked on Net-a-porter.com). I paired it with flat thong sandals and big sunglasses and wore it when we were filming *Coleen's Real Women* in Ibiza. It was a great summer look for me. Longer, fresh cotton styles worn with a big, tan-coloured, leather belt are also a look that I like, while silky shifts are great for evening. One of the nicest ones I saw was at Warehouse: it was cream with a lovely blue and red Paisley pattern on it. It must have been popular with everyone else, too, as I had to go online to get it! I also think that French Connection are really good for shift dresses.

A white cotton shift looks lovely and fresh in summer. Dress it up at night with a pair of glamorous jewel-coloured sandals

Getting the fit right

Shifts are great for those people whose figures might be slightly thicker round the middle and for anyone who has slim hips and legs. Wearing a big belt around the hips will add style – and shape – to your body, and stop your shift dress looking like a coal sack (a look I'm quite sure you will not be trying to achieve!). Fuller figures might want to try whipping out that big belt to pull the shift in at the waist – again, this gives definition and shape – while those with petite figures might choose a style that is shorter in length and that skims the body.

RIGHT Dress, Temperley London; shoes, Jimmy Choo.

Fitting the shift into your style

Mini-shifts look fantastic with bare, tanned legs, and while flat shoes are generally the best bet when wearing mini styles, wedges look great with them, too. Opaque black tights and platform shoes can look quite funky if you want to wear mini-shifts in winter. I'd also say that printed styles speak for themselves and probably don't need any extras. My favourite way to wear mini-shifts is in plain cream or white, which I accessorize with loads of gold necklaces and nothing else. You can also wear this kind of dress at night and do the same thing. If it's in more of a party style, though, with lots of detail at the neck or something, I wouldn't overload it because, really, the detail's in the dress. I had a beautiful cream and black shift with sequined flowers around the top half of the dress – it just looked so lovely as it was. My brother's girlfriend got a similar one from ASOS.com. Both showed me exactly why dresses are a one-stop style fix.

Wearing platforms with a shift gives it a more on-trend look.

✿ ABOVE Photograph © Dave M. Benett/Getty Images.

✿ Shoes, Yves Saint Laurent.

✿ RIGHT Dress, ASOS.

THE GODDESS
Perfect for grown-up glamour

Grecian-style dresses always seem to be in fashion and this draped-dress look is really one of my all-time favourites. Jennifer Lopez seems to like it a lot as well, and I love looking at those beautiful, long gowns she wears when she is photographed on the red carpet.

I think it's the soft caramel and blush colours these dresses come in that also makes me like them – they're just so classic and simple-looking. No wonder they are called Goddess dresses: the way the draped fabric moves so nicely on your body; the way your shoulders are on show, and the fact that they seem to highlight all your best bits, can certainly make you feel like a goddess! Topshop have a few variations on this style, and I saw a great goddess dress by Love Label in the Littlewoods Direct catalogue (where Amanda Wakeley also does a line). All Saints do ones that can be dressed up or down, and I'd also try ASOS.

Getting the fit right

Draped dresses look great on tall, petite or straight-up-and-down figures. All the folds of fabric and gathering that are the basis of these designs can make a curvier figure look fuller, but if the dress has a plunging neckline and good structure at the bust it can look really nice and sexy. Someone like Beyoncé carries it off brilliantly. Anyone with a small waist and fuller hips can also wear this look well. The goddess dress is maybe not the one I'd pull on if I was having a 'sticky-out-stomach' day, but I really wouldn't be put off, as that's not to say that if you don't have a straight shape and you see one you like that you shouldn't try it on (think of how great J Lo, with her famously curvy bum, looks in them); I'm just pointing out the pitfalls. So do try it on in different styles: you'll know yourself whether it's a look you feel comfortable wearing.

Fitting the goddess dress into your look

I think that this is a lovely, classic look that's great for summer. During the day I'd wear a shorter, on-the-knee style in a neutral colour – like grey, coral or sand – and dress it up with some gold jewellery. Or I might wear a gold arm cuff studded with coloured stones, like jade or turquoise. I'd probably wear flat sandals with a fine thong in gold or natural leather, and a belt to match.

During the day I'd wear a short, draped style in a soft tone like coral or sand.

If I was wearing this look at night, I'd definitely go for a longer, maxi style, as I like full-length dresses and I think they work well for formal occasions. In fact, the Temperley London dress that I wore to the Beckhams' Full Length and Fabulous party had elements of this look. I wore heels to add height, and I'd say that if you do the same it's important that the dress is long enough so that only your toes show when you are walking. If it's too short, the dress will take on a whole new look of its own and lose the classic, draped effect. The aqua-marine colour of my Temperley London dress was perfect for evening, and Boodles lent me a stunning jewelled necklace that night, which, I thought, was just the right side of bling. I had my hair pulled up in a classic bun shape, but I think long, loose waves look good, too.

Dress, Amanda Wakeley.

THE SHIRTDRESS
Perfect for everyday chic

Shirtdresses give you that classic 'effortless chic' look – someone like Claudia Schiffer might wear one with just a pair of great sunglasses and a smart structured handbag. Shirtdresses are brilliant for those days when you want to be smart but a little casual, too, and styles that sit just above the knee are definitely the most elegant. A shirtdress can look classically sexy, making it a good day-to-night outfit: I'd just add wedges or a nice round-toe court shoe in tan or some flat sandals and a wide belt to dress it up. Or I'd go for a thinner patent belt with gold detail on it.

Getting the fit right

The main thing with a shirtdress is not to wear it too tight or too baggy. If it's too tight the buttons will pull open and you don't want to expose more than you bargained for; if it's too loose, it can swamp your shape. If shirt shapes tend to fit you round the back but pull at the bust, wear a lace-trimmed camisole or vest underneath. If you've got a leaner, straight-up-and-down body shape you'll look great in a shirtdress: try hoisting it up at the hips slightly with a hipster belt.

Fitting the shirtdress into your look

Because you can button it up or button it down, you can make the dress work for winter or summer. I'd maybe wear a nice khaki-coloured one with a big brown belt and some brown leather wedges in warmer months. Or if I was to do a fresh, mini look for day, I'd only wear flats. Try Gap and Principles for classic styles that you can dress up year after year and which won't date.

GET SHIRTY

Dress, Hennes; belt, Sport Max; bangle, Topshop; clutch,
Hennes; sandals, Gap.

THE FLORAL DRESS

Perfect for real romantics

A few years ago I didn't have any floral dresses in my wardrobe. Now they are a big theme in the designer collections every spring and summer, and now I've got quite a few! And I must say, I do think all these pretty pinks, purples and citrus shades that you see on the catwalks always look so Boho and lovely. But it's with the softer, smaller, spriggy tea-dress styles that I could easily get into 'nan-dress' territory, so I have to be careful with the dress shape I choose. I'd probably go for bigger, more graphic prints, like a Marc by Marc Jacobs white mini-shift with giant flowers on it. Gucci have also done some good flower designs, and Temperley London always do something a little different with floral prints that I like, too. The Balenciaga one that I wore for the races was quite a bold look and I felt great in it.

Real Style Note

- Floral dresses need a bit more edginess to stop them looking the wrong side of old-fashioned. Some people like to wear them with leggings and flats.

- Most of the high-street stores do floral dresses every spring. Oasis are particularly good as they do some nice strapless ones with bold prints that have a more stylish and less frumpy look.

- You can find some pretty vintage dresses if you look around charity shops – it only takes a wide belt to make them look fresh and modern.

- Most dresses look great when worn with wedges and slingbacks – but I'd steer clear of black shoes with summer styles as they'll look too heavy against light colours and floral prints.

Getting the fit right

Mini-shifts with bold prints are a great look for anyone with good legs. The ones I've worn even felt fine with my shorter legs. If you're tall, you can get away with longer, floaty styles. But if you're curvy or short, traditional tea-dress shapes – buttoned up, in at the waist and out at the hip – might make you look a bit like a dinner lady. Just don't add overalls!

Fitting the floral dress into your style

Wearing tea dresses can be a hard look to pull off, and if I was going to wear one, I'd probably do it in a Boho kind of way – longer, buttoned down, with loads of accessories. Big chunky belts, flat sandals and lots of necklaces and bangles would pep the look up, too. Other ways to cut out the frump factor is to buy one with thin, Seventies-style tie straps.

Dress, Warehouse.

jeans

Jeans

Skinnies, flares, high-waisted or boyfriend – which styles are best for you?

With so many styles, colours and fits to choose from, is it just me, or has shopping for a pair of jeans become a bit of a challenge?

To be honest, I've always found it hard to get jeans that are a good fit, and I've spent a long time trying to find the perfect pair. I'm still not sure that they exist but after trying on skinny, high-waisted, boy-cut and umpteen other shapes, sizes and colours, it's fair to say I've got a good idea of what's out there now.

So what kind of jeans shape will suit you best? That's up to you. I say, if you feel good in skinnies, wear them; or if you fancy giving high-waisters a go, just do it – that's what I do. The main thing with jeans is to just try loads of pairs on: you'll know yourself what works and what doesn't. Here are my top tips on what's out there and how to wear them.

PREVIOUS PAGE Top, Marlene Birger; jeans, Earnest Sewn; shoes, Christian Louboutin.

MODERN CLASSIC

If you don't like skinnies, try straight leg
instead. Wear with a pair of cool wedges.

Top, Gap; jeans, River Island; wedges, River Island.

My jeans rulebook

1 Dress the part

When you're getting ready to go out shopping for jeans, be sure to put on the kind of top or tops that you intend to wear with them; I'd also take a good belt, too. If I'm wearing flats, I'll shove a pair of heels in my bag, or vice versa. I like a big bag for daytime, so carrying shoes around is not usually a problem for me!

Take whatever you think you'll wear your jeans with most, basically. It may sound like a hassle, but honestly, a little bit of planning works wonders, and I just think that jeans are such a big part of your wardrobe that it's worth putting the effort in.

Jeans are such a major part of our wardrobes that it's worth buying different styles for different occasions.

Jeans, Boohoo.com.

2 Don't think 'size', think 'shape'

The trick is to find a pair of jeans that highlight your best bits: you can always cover up your not-so-good parts. And remember, the sizing from one brand to the next can be completely different; so don't think size, think shape. I have some Balenciaga jeans which I love because they are really thin and stretchy and make my legs look much longer, but they are a little less flattering around my bum, as they make it look a bit long too – and with my short legs, my bum isn't long! But they do look nice with a floaty blouse that covers my bum, and I wear them all the time.

So, the trick is to think about balance and to use a few styling tricks. If you find a pair of jeans that make your bum and legs look great but that are a little loose around the waist, spend a little more on a good belt: it will pull them in and add extra style. The only definite no-no for me is when jeans are too tight at the waist, as this can give that wobbly spare tyre – or 'muffin' – look. I'd definitely go a size up in the jeans if this is the case: you wouldn't believe how much more flattering they can turn out to be.

And don't be put off by magazine articles that say a certain shape is not for you. If you like skinnies, wear them – you'll soon find your own ways of making them work; whether it's by wearing heels to add height, or pairing them with a jacket length that covers your bum and hips. Just do what I do: try, try, and keep trying until you find a pair that makes you feel good.

3 How do I get the length right?

I think that one of the most important things to get right with jeans is the length. Most of us wear high-heeled shoes with jeans now, and if your jeans are just a tiny bit short it can have a major effect on the rest of your look: if you're tall, it can make you look gangly, and if you're shorter, it can make you look stumpy.

So when you're wearing classic straight or bootcut shapes, you don't really want to see too much of the heel of your shoe. This is when taking a pair of heels with you when you go shopping is really helpful, but also take a couple of pins, too, to help you get the right length and see if the leg shape is right for you. I'll spend ages getting the hem right: I like to wear my jeans with the back of the hem just a millimetre or two off the ground – almost skimming the ground but not quite.

I apply the same rule if I'm wearing flats, too. Skinnies don't look so bad with the hem ruched up at the bottom and worn with some flats (even though my brother says I look like a stump like that).

4 Mix and match

I think it's a really good idea to have different pairs of jeans for different occasions: I'll wear some pairs going to my mum's for Sunday lunch, or for going out shopping; or I'll dress others up with a nice top if I'm meeting my mates for a drink at night. I keep my 'going out' jeans for night-time only, because if I don't wear them that often, the colour doesn't fade and they always look smart. I've also got pairs with hems a little bit longer for wearing with heels or wedges and others that are hemmed just right for wearing with flats.

If you're lucky enough to have found some jeans that do it all for you, I'd be tempted to buy a few pairs of the same style in different colours. I found a pair of dark blue J Brand ones that I liked, so I went back and bought the black ones and I also ended up getting them in a lighter blue, too. They've all got a different look and I can dress them up or down to suit wherever I'm going, but because I always feel great in them, at least if they decide not to do the same jeans next season, I'm sorted with my favourite fit.

Polka-dot tops always look great with jeans.

Blouse, Boohoo.com.

Style Tip

Department stores tend to have a good selection of designer or top denim brand styles, but if your nearest one doesn't, go online. (See my Real Style File on page 264 for the best sites for up-to-the-minute styles.)

5

Is it worth splashing out on expensive jeans?

I do wear a lot of high-street-brand jeans – Topshop skinny blacks are a great fit and they do some great bootcut ones in dark denim – but I also have pairs in my wardrobe that I have spent a little bit more on. I know that some jeans are a ridiculous price now, and I wouldn't recommend that anyone run out and buy them at the drop of a hat, but if you are really into your jeans and you can afford to splash out occasionally, go for a quality or a designer pair. These jeans have more structure and will fit your body better, which means you'll feel amazing in them. Plus they should wash well and will last you.

Jeans, high heels and a pretty blouse make one of my all-time favourite outfits.

So, just occasionally, I'd say it's worth investing in the best. The brands I would look out for are 18th Amendment, J Brand, Sass & Bide, Made in Heaven (MiH) and True Religion. Then there is 7 For All Mankind, which do some of the most flattering bootcuts around.

Top, Marlene Birger; jeans, Earnest Sewn; shoes, Christian Louboutin.

Jeans: the style lowdown

Here's my round-up of some of the key denim styles around at the moment. Read on and find the best pair for you!

STRAIGHT

Because of their straight-up-and-down classic shape, I'd say this cut is a good bet for anyone who likes a slim-leg look but who feels that skinny jeans are too edgy for them.

A good fit for: most shapes – try different labels and brands to see which suit you best. Straights make legs look longer, but only if the hem length is right.

Wear with: high, square heels or wedges, a great tan and a brown leather belt.

Brands to try: Zara, Gap, UNIQLO, Chloé, Howies, Diesel, Wrangler.

SKINNY

I love the skinny jeans look, especially ones with zips on the sides. Stella McCartney does them, and I think they are very good for people like me who have short legs. My skinny Balenciaga ones are so fine that I can wear them almost like leggings – tucked easily into boots in winter or with a big white shirt on top in warmer months. They are just the right length for wearing with a flat shoe, reaching slightly above the ankle. I like them because they're a little dressier than normal jeans.

A good fit for: those who want to draw attention to their legs or make their legs look longer. But again, try different top combinations to make sure that they fit in with your style.

Wear with: a blouse or a floaty top can look great with skinnies. Ballet pumps or flats work for day – although they can cut you off a bit if you're short like me, in which case wear them with wedges or high-heeled sandals. At night, wear high, high heels for a super-glam – and super-leggy – look.

Brands to try: Miss Sixty, Topshop, Juicy Couture, J Brand, New Look, Diesel, Sass & Bide, Superfine.

BOYFRIEND

This loose-cut, straight style is great for those who don't like the idea of skinnies but who like a lean cut that fits around the bum and waist. These jeans have a casual look, which makes them great for just pulling on at the weekend.

A good fit for: those who want to show off their bums. They can really flatter slim-hipped figures, too.

Wear with: a loose white cotton shirt or a vest and a great tan belt; or add prettiness with a loose chiffon, floral blouse. Wear plimsolls or Converse trainers, sandals or wedges.

Brands to try: ASOS, Gap, French Connection, UNIQLO, Diesel, Miss Sixty. Mango do nice ones as well.

A peasant-style floral top adds feminity to boyfriend jean styles.

 Top, ASOS.

HIGH-WAISTED

I've got a few pairs of high-waisted, wide-leg jeans. Admittedly, getting the right fit was tricky: I had to make sure that the balance between the shape at the waist and the wideness of the leg was just right. I finally found a pair of 18th Amendment ones. They were such a nice fit that I've worn them loads and I've even bought them in another colour.

A good fit for: pear-shaped or curvier figures. If you have a straight up-and-down figure and smaller hips, you're better off trying the flared style. I think high-waisters are one of the hardest fashions to pull off, though, so you'll have to decide whether to persevere with them.

Wear with: a blouse or vest tucked in at the waist; this is my favourite look. Wedges look great with high-waisters, too.

Brands to try: Sass & Bide, UNIQLO and Topshop for skinny high-risers; Cavalli, Chloé, Superfine, Gap, Topshop, French Connection, Hudson, J Brand, Radcliffe, Oasis, Mango and 18th Amendment.

❀ Wedge shoe, Faith.

BOOTCUT

I'd say most people have a favourite pair of bootcut jeans in their wardrobes. Darker washes are, I think, the most flattering, and I would steer clear of a bleach-front detail as these can make your thighs look big.

A good fit for: most shapes, but keep the hem long and wear them with heels. If your bum is not your favourite bit, though, I'd suggest you give bootcuts a miss and instead go for straight or trouser-shaped jeans. Or, give your figure good balance by choosing a more subtle flare.

Wear with: blouses, or plain vests and nipped-in jackets. Some sort of heel is a good idea, as the flared hem shape of bootcuts can make you look shorter if you are wearing flats. Converse and round-toe boots will look great with these, though.

Brands to try: Topshop, 7 For All Mankind, Gap, Diesel, J Brand, Citizens of Humanity, Next, DVB.

CROPPED

Cropped styles are brilliant for summer, or for taking on holiday, especially in white or black.

Cropped jeans look great with a stripy vest top and pumps in summer.

50

A good fit for: anyone – I'm sure there's a style out there to suit your shape. Just remember rule number 2 in my jeans rule book: try on different styles and find a fit that's right for you.

Wear with: just about anything – blouses, T-shirts, vests. Flats and elegant heels will look great with these jeans: I'd maybe wear a classic pump, or my Lanvin flats.

Brands to try: True Religion, Topshop, Gap, Oasis, Mango, Dorothy Perkins, Next, UNIQLO, Juicy Couture, Alexander McQueen, Stella McCartney, Rock & Republic.

COLOURED

I think coloured jeans sit on the fine line between good taste and bad, but if you like a different look, you can make this work. Fearne Cotton does the coloured-jeans look really well: she's got that funky take on it.

A good fit for: anyone who wants to highlight their legs and hips. Skinny coloured jeans are easier to carry off than straight or bootleg, which can look mumsy in coloured cotton. Those in a finer material, like the Balenciaga ones with ankle-zip that I wear (they come in blue, red and white) are a bit more dressy.

Wear with: pumps with a metallic finish. Accessorize the look with stacked thin bangles, or wear a blazer and a loosely wrapped scarf for a rock-chick look.

Brands to try: Topshop, UNIQLO, True Religion, See by Chloé, Balenciaga, Chloé.

❀ Vest top, Republic.

tops

Tops

A seriously pretty top can create a great look in an instant.

Whether it's a fresh, cotton blouse, a sparkly vest or a stripy sweater, a well-chosen top can completely change your look. There's such a brilliant selection of tops out there right now that none of us has to rely on just our favourite T-shirts any more. I admit, nothing looks fresher than a white vest and jeans in summer, but I think there are so many good reasons not to just reach for your favourite tee or sweater every day.

One of the handiest styling tips that I've learned lately is that creating a great look on your top half is all down to detail. But, again, I would say that the best tops for you are the ones that suit your shape, and that you feel most comfortable in. So, plain or patterned, simple or smart, in this chapter I'll suggest many ways to dress your tops up or down to suit your style, and explain how to create a practical but pretty collection of classic tops – including some great jackets – to wear with your jeans, skirts and trousers.

PREVIOUS PAGE Blouse, Marlene Birger.
RIGHT Top, Boohoo.com.

Everyday favourites

T-shirts, vests and racer-backs

SIMPLY GORGEOUS

When choosing T-shirts, I go for finer, looser styles that you can shape with a belt, or close-fitting designs like a simple vest. I love vests with shorts and skirts. If my skin's nicely tanned, I might wear a brightly coloured vest, or if I'm wearing a simple white one I'll drape some fine gold chains around my neck.

JEAN GENIUS

Tanks and racer-backs can look great with jeans. I've seen Scarlett Johansson do this look in a simple, stylish way; with some three-quarter-length denim capri pants and a plain white, cotton vest. Her gorgeous curvy figure brought a real old-fashioned sexiness to the look that made me think of the Pink Ladies in *Grease*.

A little extra detail on a vest top adds extra style.

Photograph © Peter Macdiarmid/Getty Images.

EXTRA PRETTY

If you can do that Fifties kind of thing, it can look really cute, but I'd say you have to be careful with vests as they can easily slip into 'builder' territory, and if they don't suit your shape, the effect can be a little too masculine. Layering a fine cotton shirt on top of a vest will help avoid this. Remember, too, to go for nude-coloured bras under white vests, so that they don't show through. It's nicer not to have bra straps showing, so go for tank-shaped vests, which should cover them.

SUPER SMART

Another thing I look for in a T-shirt is good-quality fabric: silk or fine cotton adds a smartness that stops a tee feeling too loose and casual, while a little more detail will look dressier. It's just the kind of thing that Joseph, See by Chloé and Topshop Unique do really well – they take a great basic T-shirt shape and make it in a luxurious or silky material. I often spend a little extra on smart T-shirts, and I find that those are the ones that last longer and wash up really well.

ALL IN THE NAME

I'm not as keen as I used to be about logos on clothes. Small ones are fine, but you have to be careful with large logos. Saying that, I remember about 13 years ago I had a pair of red Moschino jeans with 'Moschino' written all over them. I thought they were fab at the time!

Real Style Note

- If you're curvy, go for fitted tops that show off your shape.

- If you're worried about your tummy, pick a looser style with sleeve detail and a low-cut or buttoned neckline to draw attention away from it.

- If you're tall, choose a vest to highlight your waist and wear it with a fitted jacket of the same length. Elle Macpherson looks great in this combination.

- If you like to cover your bum, choose a tee with sleeve and neck detail – like a ruffle – to draw attention away from the bits you feel conscious of. I'd also try wearing longer styles that skim your hips.

Blouse, Wallis.

All-time classic

The white shirt

White shirts never go out of fashion – whether you wear one to the office every day or buy one every summer, there are not many people I know who don't wear one at some point. The good news is that they don't just come in straight 'office' styles anymore. Stores like Gap, Marks & Spencer and Hennes do several versions of classic white shirts now, as do most of the big designers. Chanel always do quite special ones, but I like the Chloé shirts, as they always have something more going on – like pleats around the neckline – and this stops them looking and feeling too stiff. I'd tend to stick to this type of shirt for during the day, but really, the brilliant thing about a white shirt is that it goes with almost anything. The key is to keep it as pristine and as white as you can; once it loses its sharpness you'll need to buy a new one.

Style Tip

Choose a crisp, fitted white blouse for a polished look or a looser, softer, hippy style for casual days. Pull your shirt in at the waist with a wide tan or black belt for a sleeker look.

Dressing the part

Beautiful blouses

I love silky or chiffon blouses. I might go for a chiffon one that's nicely fitted around the body but that has big, full or puffy sleeves. This can look just as lovely and glamorous with a pencil skirt or some high-waisted jeans as it would with classic trousers or a skirt. Smock styles with jewels and stones around the neckline can also work during the day, and short-sleeved blouses tend to look better in daytime, too.

NIGHT BRIGHTS

For night, choose loose, wide-neck blouses that sit slightly off the shoulder, as they can look just the right side of sexy – as can pussy-bow necklines and ruffle-front styles. I'd say that a plain blouse in a lush fabric and a bright or block colour doesn't need anything extra with it, as the brightness speaks for itself. I'd also stick to the same rule of 'don't accessorize' when it comes to printed styles.

IN THE MIX

Another good look to bear in mind is combining the two and wearing an evening-style top with jeans in the day. I got a fantastic silver-sequined, T-shirt-style blouse with a bow at the neck that I wore in the first series of *Coleen's Real Women*. It was from Topshop and I think it looked kind of trendy and not too blingy. I wear it with my skinny denims and high shoes. For me, this worked because I let the top do the talking and I didn't wear any accessories. I got loads of compliments on it.

A sheer, silk blouse with ruffle-front detail is just the right side of sexy.

Blouse, Marlene Birger.

The soft touch

Easy knits

Knitted tops can be quite hard to wear: they tend to be what we reach for in between seasons when it starts to get a little colder. But in changeable weather, jumpers can feel too bulky and fine-knit tops can feel too thin. My advice is: try layering.

THE WARM UP

In winter, layer a chunky-knit cardigan over your favourite long-sleeved T-shirt or polo neck. Big knitted cardigans have more shape than jumpers, which not only look better on all figures, but they give you the chance to turn the heat up or down by taking your cardi off when you're indoors.

PLAIN SAILING

In spring or summer, layer fine cotton-knit tops. Try soft colours like grey and powder-pink in cashmere or merino wool: they can look great over a plain vest. Varying the lengths of your tops worn together also gives a flattering, layered look.

GET UP AND GO

I love sweater dresses but I'm not that into big, bulky jumpers, as they can look quite shapeless, so unless I'm just nipping out or walking the dog in winter, I tend not to wear them. But plain wool V-necks and turtlenecks always have a classic smart look, and they're great for those days when you don't have much time to get ready.

A striped, sleeveless knitted top is a great option for late summer days.

Top, George at Asda.

TAKE COVER

Striped sweaters, in classic navy and cream or navy and red, can look smart with jeans in spring. I'd also invest in a nice cashmere cardi for summer nights, or a cardi-coat for autumn. Pringle and Missoni do some great knits and all the high-street faves seem to have a much wider pick of knitted tops from season to season. Topshop do some great sleeve shapes: from short, ruffle styles to wide tunic shapes; and French Connection do some great Eighties-style knitted tops in bold colours and prints. I like Joseph knits, and always try Gap for some fine cotton-mix sweaters in summer. Choose soft, muted colours – they look lovely at this time of year.

All my fave high-street shops have some great knits each season.

Short and sharp

Great jackets

Just like a lovely blouse, a smart jacket can create an instant look. Although I think some people wear fitted styles really well – Sienna Miller looks great in blazer styles – I'm not sure that tailored jackets suit my shape. I do try them on occasionally, and I did buy a Stella McCartney one once, but I think I prefer more casual styles.

So, while girls like Sienna would wear a plain blazer, a short leather jacket would be my preferred option. I've got a gorgeous Gucci one in a mushroomy colour that I wear a lot, and it looks great with a white shirt and black skinny trousers during the day. I've also got a black one that smartens the whole look up a bit. I know they are expensive, but a leather jacket is one of those investment buys that will last you a long time. And, if it's a really nice shape and made of that super-soft leather, you'll be able to wear it for years and it won't feel out of date.

Some cropped jackets with wider sleeves or blouse-like styles are also a good choice for anyone who, like me, is not so sure about blazer-style jackets.

ABOVE Photograph © Mark Campbell/Rex Features.

Jacket, Next.

A cropped jacket
gives casual looks a
cool edge.

A jewelled or sequinned jacket will inject instant glam to evening styles. Look out for them in vintage stores.

✿ Jacket, vintage.

daywear

Daywear

Everyday looks can be tricky to pull off. Here are my tips for making them work.

I do like to look groomed, but that doesn't mean that I want to be constantly dressed up every day: if I were, I wouldn't enjoy that special feeling I get when it comes to glamming up at night. The fact is, sometimes I make a big effort and sometimes I just don't. And I'm definitely not one of those girls who thinks, 'Oh, I've got the paparazzi on the doorstep, so I'll have to put on something nice'. I do love the fact that you can have two separate styles, though: you can have a night look and a day look, and both give you the chance to try out different things.

We'll look at real glamming up further on in the book, but in this chapter I'm going to show you how to add a little extra something to your daywear. I'll also look at some options for those days when any form of dressing up is just not going to happen, and totally chilling out is the only thing on your mind. Don't forget to check out my Real Style File at the back of the book for tips on where to find these styles.

 PREVIOUS PAGE Coat, Chloé.

 RIGHT Dress, River Island; bangles, Hennes.

Smart-casual

Mixing and matching styles

The key to creating any stylish daywear look is to wear a combination of smart and casual clothes. Here are some quick tips on how to do it:

How to ... keep it smart on top, casual on the bottom:

I love wearing my favourite skinnies tucked into my boots and a girly, floaty blouse on top. By adding a really nice gold belt and some gold hoop earrings, the whole outfit feels comfortable and smart.

How to ... keep it smart on the bottom, casual on top:

I do like my skirts for daytime, so if I wore something smarter on the bottom, like a tulip skirt, I might pair it with a simple coloured vest top or a T-shirt. If it's colder, I might cover up with a biker-style jacket in supersoft leather, or a fine-knit cardigan, pulled in at the waist with a thin belt.

How to ... add a hint of glamour to your day:

One of my favourite things to do with daywear is to pair some things you'd never quite imagine working together – like a glam sequin top with jeans, or a pair of great heels with jeans and a tee.

Top, Reiss; jeans, Earnest Sewn.

Key day looks

1 Black and white

An everyday classic

Whether it's a black pencil skirt and a white vest, or a white trench coat and a pair of black cigarette pants (those straight trousers that taper in to just above the ankle), I love the slickness of black-and-white combinations. Jennifer Aniston does this look so well – I'm not really one for smart trousers, but I do like the way that she will wear straight black pants with a plain white, silk T-shirt.

How to style it

Wear a loose white shirt belted in at the waist with a big black belt over some black skinny jeans. Or keep it simple in a black and white dress. Finish off with some high-heeled black wedges and a slouchy black handbag for added style.

When to wear it

For a special lunch date or when you're really not sure what to wear for an occasion. This combination works anywhere.

Go for the bold-print option: it's an easy choice and a ready-made look.

RIGHT Dress, Boohoo.com.

2 Safari

Smart city chic

OK, this is what the glossies call it but, honestly, it's not as exotic or as grown-up as it sounds, and don't worry, you don't have to be on safari to wear it! Basically, this look is all about mixing jackets, shirts, dresses and shorts in nice neutral colours like khaki, sand and white. The way I've done it before is with a pair of wide, khaki, knee-length shorts and a couple of layered tops – a sheer linen blouse and a white Marks & Spencer vest. I accessorized with a thin beige scarf and a long gold chain. My dark brown, leather handbag gave the look a city feel.

How to style it

Try wearing a khaki shirtdress with a big brown canvas belt and some gold Roman sandals. A plain white top with sandy coloured shorts and some raffia wedges will also look quite sexy, and always smart.

When to wear it

For sipping drinks outdoors with your mates in summer, or just add matt black tights and fine T-shirt layers for work in winter.

 Waistcoat, top, skirt and belt, ASOS.

 RIGHT Top, Givenchy.

3 Colour flash

Bold and bright

I love this idea; that your outfit is all one colour except for one item, whether it's your top, your shoes or your handbag. I've got a bright-yellow vest that I wear with a black pencil skirt and some black patent shoes. Or, I might be all dressed in black but I'm carrying a bright pink clutch bag. I think Marc Jacobs does the 'colour flash' thing beautifully with his collections.

How to style it

Try putting on a bright-pink blouse with black skinny jeans and boots in winter. Or wear a bright-red patent belt over a neutral-coloured dress.

When to wear it

When shopping on a Saturday or when popping out to the hairdresser. This is a look that's great for when you don't have much time: if you're all in black, just grab a brightly coloured bag.

4 Nautical
Everlasting summer style

Blue, white and red – and stripy combinations of all three – are the colours that make this really fresh. The key here, though, is to add just a hint of sailor style. For instance, Topshop did a lovely navy T-shirt dress with brass rivets around the neck and a piece of navy rope threaded through them. It was so simple. Brigitte Bardot used to pull off the nautical look in a simple way when she was younger and sailing around St Tropez. Her classic stripy, long-sleeved sailor top and white cigarette pants is one of my all-time favourite styles. But then there are loads of ways you can make this look work that will never go out of fashion.

How to style it

If you like wide-legged trousers, try wearing them with a navy vest and a red patent belt. Or, go for a short, fitted, stripy blazer with navy or red piping. Even a plain white dress with a rope-effect belt would work. And a big canvas bag with red or blue stripes is a great way of adding a touch of sailor style to any wardrobe.

When to wear it

When you want to get in a spring mood after the long winter days.

Use accessories, such as a pair of earrings, to add just a hint of sailor style to your look.

Earrings, Freedom at Topshop.

RIGHT Dress, Stella McCartney.

5 Romantic

Lovely and fresh

Ruffles, frills and pretty details will never be out of fashion in my house. Nothing says girly more than these flouncy touches. One of my favourite ever outfits was a tiered Chloé skirt in a caramel colour, which I wore with an off-white organza top with an embroidered neckline. It sounds a bit much, but the soft colour tones gave it a perfect daytime feel.

How to style it

Wear a softly coloured shirt with ruffle-sleeves and jeans. (Go for a softer, waterfall ruffle if you feel the flounced ones are too fussy.) This looks good on dresses, too.

When to wear it

When you want to feel and look totally girly.

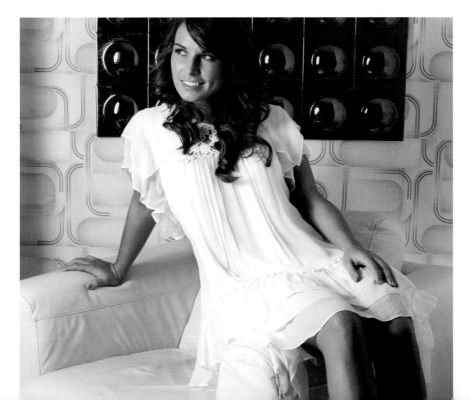

Everyone loves a hint of romance!

81

Five easy day pieces

Some things, as they say, never go out of fashion, and these five key pieces can be mixed and matched to make a whole number of daytime looks. My advice is: buy well, look after them and you'll get a whole lot of wear out of them.

A CLASSIC MAC

Short or long, black or tan, macs are a great all-rounder for spring and autumn days, and they go just as well with jeans and flats as they do with skirts and heels. From Burberry to Hennes, everyone does them.

TIMELESS PANTS

I love plain cropped or cigarette-pant styles with ballet pumps or flat sandals in the summer. Make sure the trousers cut off at exactly the right point, though – just a couple of inches above the ankle is the most flattering hemline. Gap are good for these styles, and Marks & Spencer often have them in, too.

Take good care of classic pieces and you'll get a whole lot of wear out of them.

ABOVE Photograph © Olycom SPA/Rex Features.

EVERYDAY BLACK BOOTS

I've got a pair of Marc Jacobs black suede boots that I pull out every year. The suede can get a bit worn, but I put them in the dry cleaners and they come back looking like new. Topshop always do great boots, and Office and Kurt Geiger have good selections as well.

A GREAT HANDBAG

I'd spend a little bit extra on a good black bag: it goes with anything and it doesn't wear as much as other coloured bags. Tan and white leather bags can look great for a while, but I find that they both crack and get dirty eventually. A black bag with metal buckles is always a safe choice. Make your nearest department store a first stop for a good bag. Try Karen Millen and Russell & Bromley for well-priced smart ones.

KILLER SUNGLASSES

Sunglasses can be expensive – especially for the amount of time you wear them in this country. I don't tend to wear them that often, but I've always got a good pair of Ray-Bans in my bag, just in case. Harvey Nichols has one of the best sunglasses selections, and Sunglass Hut has a good range, too. I often buy my glasses duty-free at airports.

 Sunglasses, Linda Farrow Vintage.

Lounge lover

Chilling out and still looking good.

I do make an effort to dress well most days, but sometimes at the weekend or in the evenings I just like to stay at home and curl up on the sofa. Some people like to wear jeans and a jumper on lazy days, but to me jeans are not very comfortable and that's why Juicy Couture trackies are always my favourite lounging outfits. I know they are not the most flattering things, but I'm not too fussed about dressing up every day if I don't need to.

But that doesn't mean to say that when I'm pottering around at home that I'm happy to look like someone who just walked off the local building site in search of a bacon buttie. And that's good because, Juicy's aside, you can now get a great choice of loungewear that is lovely and comfortable, yet smart enough not to frighten any visitors or family who happen to pop by. Here are a few of my favourite ideas for what to wear when chilling out:

THE WARM UP

There's nothing like the feel of soft cashmere against your skin, and it's just the thing for snuggling up on the sofa. Lots of cashmere companies now do loungewear ranges in nice colours that include pieces like roll-top trousers and hoodies. Marks & Spencer and Gap do some nice stuff, but if you don't want to splash out, get a nice big sweater from the menswear department at George at Asda or Tesco, and wear it with leggings and ballet pumps.

LOVELY, LAZY DAYS

Rather than buy cheaper leggings (which can go baggy really quickly), splash out on some that are made from better-quality fabric and that are not too strongly elasticated at the waist: they'll hold you in a little more, will feel comfortable and will wash up well. There are many wide-leg choices out there, too: Gap do some great ones, in plain and patterned styles and in different types of cotton. Online companies, such as Hush and The White Company, are also good for this kind of thing, and they often stock roll-top versions, which pull you in a bit more at the waist. Also try Net-a-porter and Benetton for leggings.

KEEPING IT SIMPLE

Sweater dresses are perfect for pottering around the house in – and I'd be happy to leave the house in one if I had to pop out. On a really cold day, I might wear mine with a nice big scarf wrapped loosely around my neck for extra warmth and style. In summer, a long, tunic-style T-shirt is great for slipping over leggings or wide-leg pants; and a nice, fine-knit, long-sleeved tee can make trackie bottoms look smarter. Hush do a great range of loungewear. Check out the Real Style File on page 263 for where to find this company.

lingerie

Lingerie

From pretty everyday wear to perfect special-occasion sets.

Since Agent Provocateur came on the scene a few years back, underwear has become far more of a fashion thing than it used to be. This company has put a lot of cheeky fun into lingerie, and most brands seem to have taken their lead, offering some gorgeous, special pieces alongside the basic stuff.

The styles I like most, though, are everyday bra and pants that have a little something extra about them, whether it's a tiny gold satin bow in the middle of a plain white bra, or a girly polka-dot print in pastel colours. Marks & Spencer have fantastic ranges, and the Elle Macpherson Intimates collection is lovely, too.

But looks aside, the most important thing about lingerie is the fit: get this right and it will seriously make the most of your figure and heighten all the best bits of your body.

Bras are one of the things that girls always chat about. So, in this chapter, I'm going to pass on some hints that I've picked up to help you find the kind of lovely lingerie to make you look and feel your best – inside and out.

 PREVIOUS PAGE American Vintage T-shirts.

  RIGHT Underwear, from a selection at Matalan, Littlewoods and George at Asda.

Bras

The main thing is that you should be wearing a bra that really supports your bust, comfortably. If the wires are sticking into you or if you are constantly pulling up the straps, you probably need to get refitted. But whether you're small, or big, on top, the great thing about getting a well-fitted bra is that it can do wonders for your shape.

So, if you think it's time you went for a proper fitting, here are some things you might like to know before you go:

Bra too big?

If you're wearing a bra that's too big, there'll be nothing holding up your bust, making your top half look quite shapeless. If you go down a size, though, it will pull everything in a little and make your waist look more defined.

Bra too small?

If your bust is spilling out of your bra, or if you're hanging over it at the back or under the arms, you could be doing your figure a real disservice. If you go up a cup size, you'll get a really smooth line under your clothes that will make the most of your curves.

Getting the fit right

Obviously, I'm not an expert, but anything I've learned I've picked up when having fittings of my own. Department stores like Debenhams and House of Fraser are brilliant places to have fittings done.

Most of the staff on the lingerie floors are properly trained, so this means that often they can just look at you and tell whether the bra that you're wearing is the right fit. Tell them about any problems you might be having and you'll find they are always really helpful.

What to wear

If you are thinking about going for a bra fitting, it's a good idea to make an appointment first. On the day, make sure you are wearing a plain top or T-shirt that clings to your shape – that way both you and the assistant can see exactly what each type of bra is doing for your figure.

Don't be shy about this, as it will really help you to find the right fit and so can change your body shape a lot. I know it can feel a bit awkward having to whip everything off and stand in a cold cubicle while your body is being pushed about all over the place by a stranger, but a good salesperson won't make you uncomfortable and you'll feel fine in seconds. Plus, she'll bring you lots of nice bras to try on!

While one expert says you're a particular size, another might tell you something different: so it is always worth getting a second opinion.

Lingerie for Day

With stores now bringing more and more pretty everyday styles into their ranges, what better excuse do you need to spring clean your underwear drawer?

UNDER COVER: BRIEFS

By day I tend to wear a mixture of thongs and briefs; I don't find thongs that attractive, but there's no denying their practicality! If I'm wearing a dress, though, I'll wear classic briefs. Of course, then there are 'easy' days when only your most comfortable cotton knickers will do. Overall, I'd say that it's best not to stick to one style but to mix-and-match your knickers to suit the outfits you wear.

✿ Briefs, Next.

THE HOLD UP: BRAS

T-shirt bras: I just live in T-shirt bras during the day as they are nicely shaped and, because they don't have any lacy details or seams, they are invisible under close-fitting tops. Lacy bras will look bumpy under tighter tops, so I'd leave those for special occasions.

Bra tops: These styles look like cut-off vests and are a great comfort choice for girls who are smaller on top, as they don't have wires or firm straps. Sloggi do some nice ones.

Non-wired: These are good for those who don't like the 'hemmed-in' feeling of wires, or who don't need much support. Cotton-band styles or padded non-wired are a good choice. Triumph do some pretty styles.

Minimizers: The cups on these bras are said to slightly reduce the appearance of a large bust, though some girls don't like the way they flatten theirs out. The Gorgeous range at Debenhams is a good choice with some great everyday and evening styles. Freya do some of the trendiest larger-bust styles, and you can pick these up in John Lewis and other department stores.

Seamless: Apart from T-shirt styles, these are my favourites. I like the soft, silky fabric, as you really don't feel as if you're wearing a bra when you've got one on. You can also get underwired versions for more support: designer versions, like those by DKNY, are really nice. Online lingerie shop Figleaves.com has a massive range of all styles.

RIGHT Underwear, from a selection at Matalan, Littlewoods and George at Asda.

CAMISOLES

I buy loads of cotton cami-vests from Marks & Spencer, and I wear them almost every day. They are great for wearing under sheer tops and blouses, and in winter I think they are the only thing to wear under jumpers and sweaters. Gap also do some great extra-light cami-tops, and you can pick up glam ones in department stores.

Lingerie for evening

Going-out nights are your chance to wear some really special underwear, and I think it's a good idea to put on something a bit lacy, silky, or more feminine when you're getting ready to go out. You'd be surprised at how much nicer it makes you feel: it gives you instant glam factor for a start. My favourite special pieces are from La Perla and Agent Provocateur, and I love getting a chance to wear them as they are just so girly. Oasis also do a gorgeous lingerie range called Odille, and I like the Princesse Tam-Tam range, which you can get in department stores. Freya and Fantasie also have nice ranges for bigger busts, and don't forget Rigby & Peller.

SET AND MATCH

Nothing feels as glamorous as wearing a matching set of lingerie. So, if I'm going to spend money on a good night-time bra, I'll tend to splash out on the matching knickers as well. Although I'm not keen on them, G-strings or thongs are usually the most practical choice for putting on under eveningwear, as they appear invisible and do away with any unsightly knicker lines, which are always easier to see through finer fabrics. Glitzy, diamanté-studded ones are not really my cup of tea. I prefer sheer or lacy shorts styles.

Wear some lacy or silky lingerie when you're getting ready to go out: you'll feel gorgeous.

 LEFT Vintage camisole.

BEST BRAS FOR NIGHT

Multiway: I think all girls should have one of these bras in their lingerie drawer. The straps can easily be taken off to give you a halterneck bra, strapless, or a crossover back, which is ideal for cutaway-sleeve or vest-top styles. I'd steer away from those 'clear' straps that come with some of them, though, as I think they look kind of strange and not very attractive. Go for a nude colour and you'll get loads of wear out of it. Wonderbra's Multiplunge is a good choice.

Strapless: If, like me, you love strapless dresses, I'd say it's really worth investing in a decent strapless bra. It will make you feel supported and give you a nice shape around the bust-line. But make sure you don't get one that's too small, because if too much of your bust spills out, it won't be flattering and will spoil the elegant look of your dress. Fantasie do some nice smooth cup bras that would work well with most styles. Try Ballet, Fantasie and Rigby & Peller strapless styles if you have a larger bust.

Balconette and Wonderbra: These bust-enhancers are great for special nights out and they work well with fitted clothes that are lower at the neckline. Again, the trick is to get the sizing right: the idea is to give your cleavage a natural-looking boost – you don't want to look as though you've got two oranges trying to escape from your dress!

Backless/bra-less: They look a bit strange, but these 'bra-less' styles have a special tape that sticks to your body, so they're great for wearing with backless dresses or tops. Padded and underwired versions of these bras will define your shape a little more. You might find these hard to wear if you're bigger busted, though, as backless styles are unlikely to give you enough support.

 Slip, Warehouse; corsages, Johnny Loves Rosie.

accessories

Accessories

Perfect finishing touches: from scarves to handbags and high heels.

Adding necklaces, scarves and bags not only completes your outfit, but trying them out in different ways gives you a chance to really personalize what you are wearing.

Someone who does this really well is the Hollywood stylist, Rachel Zoe. She became famous for creating the whole 'LA girl' look (big sunglasses, giant bags and huge heels) that Lindsay Lohan and Nicole Richie made popular. Bold accessories are her thing, and it's because she uses them well that they really work. She just keeps it simple with just one or two accessories, and it's a look I really like.

The giant bag is definitely one of my all-time favourite accessories. If I had to choose between bags and shoes (although I hope I never do!) I'd say that big bags are my *big* thing.

But whatever your favourite pieces – the great thing about accessories is that you can have fun trying out lots of different things.

I've made a note of a good few bits of advice about how to make the most of them. So, from scarves to handbags and high heels, when it comes to the finishing touches, this chapter's got it covered.

PREVIOUS PAGE Top, Hennes; ring, vintage.

RIGHT Cocktail rings, QVC.

Pile jewelled cocktail rings on at night for
a little after-dark sparkle.

Handbags

If there's one thing that I am always happy to spend a little bit extra on each year, it's a good handbag.

I've always been into handbags, and I've got different ones to suit different outfits or events.

Everyone needs a decent, do-everything handbag, though. They're like our houses and they've usually got everything but the kitchen sink in them, too. So as you're going to use your everyday bag so much, I'd say it's worth spending a little more on a good, classic style that's going to last. Here are some of my favourite styles; I think you'll like them too.

SLOUCHY

A good, slouchy, leather bag in tan, black or brown will give you that kind of effortless style that doesn't look as though you've tried too hard. Those with metal buckles or clasps look really smart. My current faves are Yves Saint Laurent's Downtown and Chloé's Bay patent bag. Topshop and Next also do some great slouch styles.

I'm always happy to spend a little extra on a good handbag.

Handbag, Chanel.

PADDED

This is a real Chanel look and I'm surprised at how much my classic black bag with silver-chain shoulder straps goes with everything. Topshop often do styles that echo the padded look and I've seen some nice ones in department stores such as House of Fraser.

STRUCTURED AND FRAMED

Many designer bags tend to have a more solid, square shape with lots of hardware – big metal buckles and clasps. I love my black Birkin bag by Hermès but Marc Jacobs and Alexander McQueen also do a lot of framed bags. Try Karen Millen and Red Herring at Debenhams for good framed styles.

Padded styles never date – they always have real Chanel style.

COLOURED

A brightly coloured bag can really lift an all-black outfit. So if you see a bright pink one and you really love it – go for it. Don't forget, though, that you might not get as much use out of a coloured bag as other styles, so it's not worth spending too much on one. Try New Look, Coast, Topshop and Miss Selfridge for some great styles. But if you do want to splash out, Christian Louboutin have a great selection of brightly coloured ones.

OVERSIZED OR PATENT

I think a giant bag can either look fantastic or a real show, depending on how you wear it. And if you're quite small-framed, be careful that your bag doesn't look as though it's carrying you. A big patent bag can look really fashiony when you use it as the only accessory to dress up a plain outfit. Try Mulberry, Warehouse and River Island; Karen Millen also do some really nice ones.

CLUTCH

There are loads of brilliant clutch bags in the shops now. From plain black in luxury fabrics like satin and snakeskin-effect, you can get a bag that will go with every kind of evening outfit. Accessorize is one of my favourite places to pick up those styles, and I've also got a patent Chanel clutch that I often use if I'm just going for drinks with the girls. It dresses up jeans really well. Ted Baker and New Look do some great clutches too.

Evening bag, Coast.

Shoes

Maybe it's something to do with my being short, or it could be that there are just so many amazing shoes to choose from every season, but I love everything about heels: they just make you feel instantly better, taller, and more feminine. Christian Louboutin is my all-time favourite shoe designer. But although I wear high heels a lot, there are some days when you just need something comfortable, so I've got my fair share of flats, boots and casual styles tucked away in my wardrobe. I take as basic an approach to choosing shoes as I do to putting together my outfits: I stick to classics, as they will usually work with lots of different looks.

FEET FIRST: HITTING THE HIGH STREET

I think shoes are one of the big areas where the high street gets it so right – you can even pick up individual styles that are not copied from the catwalks, or anyone else, and I think that's brilliant, as they have a really unique touch to them. I've got loads of high-street styles. Here are some of my favourite places to get them:

Shoes, Christian Louboutin.

My high-street shoe shopping list

Kurt Geiger

Kurt Geiger shoes are fantastic, and I've bought quite a few from their Fashionista range. They are not always that cheap, but they do look individual and, unlike other high-street brands, they don't just do straight copies of shoes from the catwalks.

Russell & Bromley

I used to see Russell & Bromley shoes as being a bit too old for me, but you can get some great classic styles here that you could bring out every year without them looking dated.

Aldo

I know quite a few people who buy lots of shoes from Aldo, especially in the summer. Lots of my friends buy sandals here, and I think the styles always look great.

Office

I tend to get my Birkenstocks and Converse from Office, but they have nice little ballet pumps and flip-flops, too.

Topshop

I love Topshop shoes, and it is especially great for boots and flats. You'll get some great coloured styles here, too. A lot of the Topshop styles have a real designer feel to them.

Faith

Faith have a fantastic range of wedges. I bought a gold pair one summer that went with everything and were great for day, night and for taking on holiday. They were a real hit with me and all my friends.

Metallic looks are gaining real
classic fashion status, and a
platform pump is a subtle way
to add a hint of shine.

HEELS

For years, fashion mags have been telling us to always have a pair of black stilettos in the cupboard, and I take their point. A classic heel, yes; but I don't think it always has to be black. Here are some of my favourite styles:

PLATFORMS

My favourite heels just now are my strappy, patent, YSL platforms; they have a chunky platform sole and a high stiletto heel and they go with everything – jeans, skirts and dresses. The brown leather pairs look great in summer. All the designers and the high-street brands, from Yves Saint Laurent to French Connection and Faith, do some great platform styles, so shop around.

WEDGES

Wedges are a great all-round high heel: they look fashionable, are easier to walk in and they can make your legs look extra-long. They're also perfect for wearing in the day when a stiletto might look too much. Espadrille styles with raffia heels, or cork-heeled ones, are ideal for wearing with prettier summer colours, but there's a wide range available on the high street now and some designers are doing great ones for evening, such as metallic and patent or patterned ones, which have a little more edge. Buy a pair for day and a more glam pair for night. Karen Millen has a lovely selection.

Coloured wedges work well with pretty summer colours.

Shoes, Freemans.

FLATS

JEWELLED SANDALS

Jewelled sandals are ideal for wearing with all sorts of summer styles – from tea dresses to skirts and jeans – as they add a hint of glam but are comfortable at the same time. You'll always find good ones at Kurt Geiger and Topshop.

BALLET PUMPS

These slip-on flats never date and they are great for pottering around in the day and I have a great pair of Lanvin ones. Ballet flats look good worn with skinny jeans and three-quarter length trousers, and while plain black ones go with most things, brighter colours or different finishes, like patent, metallic or fake snakeskin, can lift your outfit. Watch out when wearing skirts and dresses, though: ballet flats with these can make everyone but the very long-legged look a little dumpy.

✿ Ballet pumps, Shellys.

LOAFERS

I thought I'd left these behind when I left school, but Chloé made loafers cool again. The best ones have a very flat sole and a very slightly raised heel. I like them because they are simple but look smart with jeans. Try colours other than black – like tan, white and mustard – as they can look more stylish. Topshop do some nice ones.

ROMAN SANDALS

Roman sandals are a great summer all-round shoe. Again, I'd say tan or metallic leather ones are more versatile, as they go well with different colours. I think fine ankle straps are most flattering and I'd probably steer clear of those ones that go too far up your leg, as it can be quite a hard look to pull off. I'd leave that to the catwalks. Office have some lovely ones.

Sandals, Gap.

Beauty Tip

Summer sandals require summer-ready feet. So, when the days start to get warmer, book yourself in for a really thorough pedicure to get rid of rough skin on heels. It will leave feet feeling soft and silky. Choose a bold nail colour to give toes a real lift, too.

FLAT THONG SANDALS

Because the thong comes between your toes and travels up the centre of your foot, it gives a nice, flattering shape so you can go as simple or as fancy as you like. The most flattering thong sandals are those that have fine straps and a little buckle at the side. Braided leather ones are ideal everyday slip-ons, and jewelled styles look gorgeous with everything. St Tropez are a good make, New Look have some nice, simple ones, and Gap usually do a great version every year.

PLIMSOLLS

I love Converse for kicking around in at home and for taking the dog out for a walk, and they may not be pretty but Birkenstocks are great for holidays. I think the natural leather thong ones look best. Try Schuh and Shellys for plimsolls and Kurt Geiger for Birkenstocks.

Plimsolls, La Redoute.

BOOTS

KNEE-HIGH

I have my favourite black, knee-high, Marc Jacobs boots that I pull out every year. The heel is not too high, so that makes them really comfortable but with just enough lift. However, classic shapes (like a round-toe boot with a stack heel) won't date and you can wear those to smarten up winter styles, or pair them with longer dresses in spring and autumn. I'd go for a tan, black or dark brown colour if you want lasting wear out of them. Go for boots that fit just below the knee and that are not too tight around the leg. Try Topshop and Next for some classic styles. Department stores like House of Fraser are also a good bet.

EVERYDAY

Loose leather or suede styles can be good with jeans and skirts, but be careful where they go to on your leg: many tend to stop halfway up the calf and this can be really unflattering on most shapes. I'd probably go for boots that skim just below the knee. Try Schuh, Shellys or Office.

ANKLE BOOTS

These have become a bit more trendy recently. I love them with jeans, and some girls, like Lindsay Lohan, can make them look quirky when worn with short skirts. But I do think you have to put a little effort into making the ankle-boots-look work. Beware of flat ones that can shorten your figure; try platform versions for a more flattering, trendy look.

I love ankle boots with jeans. They look quirky when worn with short skirts.

Belts

I think a belt is a girl's best friend. No matter what your size, a belt can give you a great shape, and from a dressy point of view a well-chosen belt will always add a special touch to any outfit.

You can get lots of great belt styles on the high street now, but I'd say it's worth investing in a good leather belt for everyday wear – you want it to last and not lose its shape. I also pick up some of the more glam high-street ones for night, as they can add a real designer touch to outfits. George at Asda has a fantastic selection of belts in neutral colours, and Reiss has some smarter, well-priced ones. I've seen some good, big, tan ones at Warehouse as well.

Real Style Note

- Loop a skinny, brightly coloured, patent belt into your jeans: it will add something extra to an everyday outfit.

- A wide belt really emphasizes the waist area and will give your body an all-round, better, more feminine shape.

- Try tying a big, wide belt over shirts or dresses at the waist. You'll be surprised at the different looks you can achieve.

- If an outfit that you've bought – a shirtdress, say – comes with a belt, swap it with one from your wardrobe or try twisting a vintage or patterned scarf into a belt for a more individual look.

- Don't always go for black on black. Tan or brown can give a more polished, individual style.

RIGHT Dress, Couture Couture.

Hats

I like those big, floppy, Seventies-style felt hats, and I think Sienna Miller has made the rock-chick trilby style her own. The hat I like the best, though, has to be the beanie. My favourite one, which I wear all winter, is from Reiss; it is black, crocheted and studded with sequins, and it adds a little bit of sparkle to my winter outfits. It's good for bad-hair days too!

Scarves

I have really taken to wearing scarves of late; you can do so much with them and they have that great smart-casual thing where you can dress up a plain look in the day, or use them as a light cover-up at night. Go for big ones that you can wind loosely round your neck, so that it kind of looks slightly stacked up. Big scarves are great for playing around with, so just try them in lots of different ways. Try different textures – fine wool, chiffon or silk – to create different looks.

Scarves can be worn in so many ways. Use them to dress up an everyday outfit or to dress evening styles down a little.

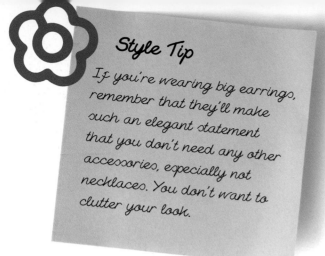

Jewellery

EARRINGS

For day, I like plain, simple diamond studs as they go with anything. Of a night, though, I love my big earrings, as they make any outfit look instantly glam. I'll tend to go for the boldest ones I can find – either big hoops or extra-long styles. Erickson Beamon do amazing styles, and they've started doing ranges for Debenhams and Kurt Geiger, too. Find them at: Mikey, Butler & Wilson and Net-a-porter. Kenneth Jay Lane, Mawi and Zoe & Morgan can all be found at Net-a-porter.

Big earrings give evening looks a super-stylish edge.

Earrings, Erickson Beamon at Debenhams.

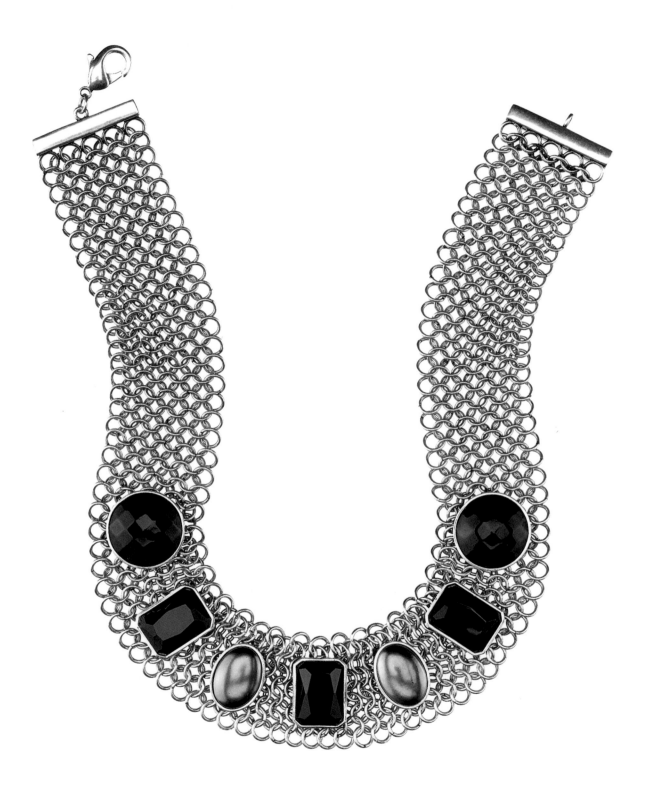

NECKLACES

I used to find necklaces hard to wear, as I was never sure whether to go for beads, chains or pendants, but again, I've just tried lots of styles. I'm not much of a beads or a pearls girl (my Chanel pearls are the exception), but I think the bold, natural-looking necklaces made of coloured stones and wood that you find in all the shops just now can look great with a plain white shirt or a vest. I also like wearing a few long, gold chains with plain styles – longer strands look better with longer dresses. But, again, if there's a lot of detail around the neckline of what I'm wearing, I'll leave necklaces out. If the neckline is plain, though, I might go for a really glamorous necklace to make a real statement. Find them at: Lara Bohinc, Butler & Wilson, Freedom at Topshop, Diva at Miss Selfridge, Mikey, Johnny Loves Rosie, Kenneth Jay Lane and Juicy Couture at Net-a-porter, Lola Rose and Erickson Beamon.

Style tip: if you're wearing chains, beads or necklaces, go for smaller earrings. Sticking to one shade of metal – either silver or gold – looks slicker than wearing a mix of the two.

✿ Necklace, Erickson Beamon at Debenhams.

RINGS

Cocktail rings are really fashionable now, and I think they're a lovely touch. I got my engagement ring made quite big, as I like that statement-ring kind of look. Loads of shops are doing them now and I think Accessorize do some of the best. Find them at: Johnny Loves Rosie, Accessorize, Freedom at Topshop, Erickson Beamon at Kurt Geiger, Diva at Miss Selfridge, Butler & Wilson, Yves Saint Laurent, Nine West and Lola Rose.

Style tip: a really big, single-stone cocktail ring will add elegance to any outfit; wear two or three for a high-fashion look.

BRACELETS AND CUFFS

Cuffs add a gorgeously glamorous edge and there are lots of places to find bracelets with expensive-looking detail on them that don't cost the earth. A nice gold cuff worn halfway up your arm looks lovely in summer and a more decorative one can look fantastic with a plain evening dress. Find them at: Erickson Beamon at Kurt Geiger, Nine West, Freedom at Topshop, Laura Lee at the Ruby Red Company, Johnny Loves Rosie and Chanel.

Style tip: go for bracelets with extra detail – wood and gold, or textured stones – for a really expensive look.

✿ RIGHT Dress, Couture Couture; ring, Coast.

✿ LEFT Cuff, Chanel.

WATCHES

I think watches are quite precious, and therefore they tend to be expensive, but they can work as a piece of jewellery in their own right. I do like wearing different watches for different things, so I've got a nice big, chunky, gold one that looks good with most things for day, and at night I'll wear a dressier, jewelled watch; maybe with some of my diamond bracelets. I have nice memories attached to my watches as they have often been given to me as gifts. They remind me of all the different events I've worn them to. Find them at: H Samuel, Argos, The Watch Hut, Swatch shops. Department stores offer a selection of classic watch brands such as Rotary and Tissot, as well as designer fashion watches from D&G, DKNY, Emporio Armani and Red Herring. If you want to invest in an expensive watch, go for a Rolex or a Cartier.

Style tip: bigger styles are best for wearing in the day – they can look too clunky and casual for evening.

Watches, Red Herring and Dreyfus & Co.

SUNGLASSES

I do like wearing sunglasses as they make outfits look so stylish, but I tend to only put them on in the summer or on holiday. Some people do that whole 'coming-out-of-the-airport-sunglasses-look' really well, but it's just not me; I'd feel a bit stupid coming out of the airport in sunglasses on a cloudy Manchester day!

My favourite styles are classic Aviator shapes, and I like the retro feel of oversized Linda Farrow Vintage ones. But I love snapping up high-street designs because they tend to be priced well so you can stock up on different pairs to go with different outfits. Find them at: Linda Farrow Vintage at Harrods, Topshop, Sunglass Hut, Zara, Next, Net-a-porter, New Look and Mango.

Style tip: summer aside, big sunglasses look great in spring and autumn when worn with skinny jeans and a classic belted mac.

Some people do that whole 'coming-out-of-the-airport sunglasses look' really well but it's just not me.

Sunglasses, Ray-Ban at Freemans.

smart dressing

Smart dressing

For work or that important first date, here's how to dress to impress.

I remember that 'first day of school' feeling when I got a Saturday job as a shop assistant in New Look. It wasn't that I was just nervous about what work was going to be like, but I wasn't sure about what to wear either – especially for working in a fashion shop! In the end, the job was great. Even better, I got a fantastic discount on all the clothes. From then on choosing my outfits was a whole lot easier.

A couple of years later, though, when I had to meet my editor at *Closer* for the first time, I had a similar butterflies-in-my stomach feeling. I had no idea what the right thing to wear might be. Smart? Casual? A mix of both? In the end, I just wore a nice Chloé day dress that I felt good in and that I think had elements of all of the above. I suppose it worked, because I got the job.

It's a real balancing act knowing what to wear when you are trying to impress. So, whether you'd like a new look for work, some ideas of how to dress for that first date, or if you're just fed up of wearing the same thing day-in, day-out, in this chapter I'll give you a whole new set of ideas on how to put together a few outfit options, along with some tips and tricks to help you make the most of your working wardrobe: a wardrobe that works for you.

PREVIOUS PAGE Dress, Philip Lim 3.1; shoes, Christian Louboutin.

RIGHT Top, Yves Saint Laurent; skirt, Joseph.

Three great date looks

1 Tried and tested

Nothing makes you feel sexier than your favourite pair of skinny jeans, and they will work just as well for a day- or a night-time date. So, wash them up until they are a snug just-out-of-the-machine fit and on top wear a nice T-shirt with some detail, like ruffle sleeves, or a printed blouse – something a little more dressy than normal. Cover up with a light trench coat or a short, fitted jacket. Ballet pumps would look nice, but make sure they're clean and smart and not too bashed about. If you're wearing heels, choose ones that you feel comfortable in and, most importantly, can walk in.

2 Hint of glam

A good sequined top or a blouse with shiny or metallic detail is a definite eye-catcher; it looks like you've dressed for the occasion but not too much, and that hits just the right note. Also, you'll shimmer a little as you move and that's no bad thing on a first date. Wear with jeans, sandals or medium-high wedges; if you prefer heels, I'd say it's best not to go for anything too high, as you don't want to feel restricted by them.

3 Dress it up

Nothing will make you feel more feminine than a dress, and if ever there's a time you want to feel like a lady, it's surely now. Take a hint from Burberry and add a stylish edge to a

Dress, ASOS; belt, ASOS.

simple shift dress with a studded belt. Or go for a nice, tiered number and wear it with a pair of roman sandals. If you want to wear heels, see the note on jeans above. Flat sandals will look nice in summer; something with a higher heel could well be your best option in winter. On the dress front, my big 'no-no' would be any dress that was too short, low-cut or revealing.

Bold colour adds real statement factor to classic dress styles.

Ten easy work pieces

1 Shirt

A good everyday shirt is a must for work, but it doesn't have to look like your old school one. Try a fitted one with short, puff sleeves. Cotton shirts with bow tie-necks are also nice for day, and some have removable ties, which means you get more options for your money and more wear out of them.

Colour-wise, I'd stick to plain black or white, or stripy, as these will easily match your other basics. If you want something a little edgier, choose a loose, silky T-shirt or vest in a neutral colour, like beige or grey. You'll always find a great selection of work shirts at: M&S Limited Collection, Topshop, French Connection, See by Chloé and Gap.

Puff sleeves and delicate buttons lift a classic white shirt – perfect for the office.

2 Trousers

Whether you're in a formal or a more casual environment, high-waisters are a more modern alternative to straight black ones. My mate got a really great pair with buttons up the front from the Freemans catalogue for £30. And while I think that jeans on a first day are generally a no-no, I do think that once you're in a job and realize the dress code is quite casual, then jeans might be okay.

If you feel you don't suit high-waisted styles, go for skinny black jeans or slouchier trousers that taper in to the ankle – they look great with platform heels. I'm not a fan of boot-cut formal trousers, but if you prefer something with more of a flare at the bottom, just remember not to wear them too short! You'll always find a great selection of modern work trousers at: River Island, Oasis, French Connection, Topshop, Jaeger, Next and Reiss.

3 Skirt

I think everyone – whatever their shape – looks great in a pencil skirt: they always look feminine, no matter what. If you go into an office every day, you can do that sassy smart look that someone like Catherine Zeta Jones would do – wearing it with a smart jacket tied with a belt at the waist, or just a short-sleeved blouse.

Another look that I think works well for the office is a tulip skirt: it has some soft gathering at the waist and then tapers in. It's not as sharply tailored as a pencil skirt, so it feels a little more causal. You can dress down any smart skirt with a casual T-shirt or vest. You'll always find a great selection of work skirts at: Reiss, Ted Baker, Topshop and Zara.

Shirt, Boohoo.com

4 Dress

You can fit almost any dress shape into your working wardrobe. But for styles that you are likely to get most wear out of, I'd stick to shifts and shirtdresses. You can make a shirtdress look as plain or as dressed up as you like: wearing it with ballet flats and a hipster belt will work in the day; while a glam belt and high heels will work for those nights you want to go for a drink after work. Go for Fifties-style knee-length shifts that follow the shape of your body and just clasp on a wide belt, or choose the shorter Sixties-style shift and wear with opaque tights and flats or wedges. You'll always find a great work dress at: Dorothy Perkins, Principles, Warehouse, Oasis, Mango, Jaeger, M&S Limited Collection and French Connection.

5 Jacket

Go for short, fitted jackets: they look modern and smart when worn with dresses, trousers and skirts. Gap do some of the best jacket styles – it's just a case of trying them on to find a fit for you. Wear open and loose and push the sleeves up for added style. If you prefer to cover your bum, go for a longer jacket and leave it open for a more casual look. Short-sleeved jackets and ones that have a blousey feel will give you a less formal look. You'll always find a great work jacket at: Topshop, Gap, New Look, Ted Baker, French Connection and Oasis.

6 Waistcoat

A waistcoat can look great with trousers and just as good with skirts and jackets. I think they look especially good with pencil skirts, as they highlight the waist and curve round the hips. It's sassy rather than sexy, and that's the perfect balance for a work outfit. Wear it with a plain vest in summer. In winter, a long-sleeved chiffon blouse would work well. Either look works with trousers – especially skinnies. If you are wearing high-waisted trousers, though, go for a shorter style of waistcoat and belt it around the waist. You'll always find a great waistcoat at: New Look, Topshop, All Saints and Miss Selfridge.

7 Structured bag

Whether you want to appear smart or casual, a structured bag – one with a frame or a square shape – will update your look. If you want your workbag to say, 'I mean business', then go for a classic Kelly shape – it looks like a feminine version of a briefcase. But if your workbag is also likely to be used at weekends, go for something a little slouchier but with metal buckles and detail to smarten it up. The Mulberry Maxi-Mabel bag in trendy blue leather is a great choice as it's a good alternative to black and has an up-to-the-minute feel. If your work bag is going to be your everyday bag, though, don't go for one that looks too severe or business-like. You'll always find a good work bag at: Next, Russell & Bromley, LK Bennett, Karen Millen, Zara, New Look, ASOS and good department stores.

Bag, Mulberry.

8 Belted mac

A classic mac never goes out of fashion, and it suits all kinds of weather. That's the great thing about a mac – you'll get so much wear out of it, so it's ideal for the office. It looks good when worn in a smart or a casual way and is loose enough to fit over a jacket on cold or wet winter days. Black, tan and navy are the most versatile colours; white looks super–chic, but remember that it's a high-maintenance colour. You'll always find a great trench at: Burberry, Gap, Topshop, Dorothy Perkins and Hennes.

9 Court shoes

There are lots of plain court shoe styles out there and most of them look as dreary as a wet Wednesday. So I'd say relegate all those big, chunky, square-toed ones into the fashion bin and choose a stylish pair. You don't have to spend a lot, but a cool-looking pair of shoes is always going to make you feel great. Platform courts are what I would choose; though I'd probably go for a nude as well as a black pair, as neutral tones go with most things and can give your outfit a bit more of an edge. Or try a patent shoe, as it will always add polish. You'll always find a great pair of courts at: Dune, New Look, Office, Aldo, Nine West and Kurt Geiger.

Add a neutral-toned pair of shoes to your work wardrobe: they'll look great with tanned legs in summer.

Style Tip

The outfit you choose for your first day at work will depend on the job that you do. We all want to make a good impression, but I think the trick is to be a bit low-key on your first day. You'll soon get the dress code and know what's right and what's not.

10 Belt

A great belt is an absolute must-have. I'd invest in three styles – a brightly coloured skinny, a wide black one with a big buckle, and a wide, natural-leather one. Each of these belts will work with most outfits and will allow you to style your work outfits in several different ways. Just adding a belt gives a slick touch to any outfit. You'll always find great belts at: department stores, Next, George at Asda, New Look, Reiss, Topshop and Warehouse.

🌸 LEFT Shoes, Marks & Spencer.

🌸 Belt, Hobbs.

Diary of a working wardrobe

Whether you spend each day in an office, restaurant or a creative environment, you can use these 10 easy pieces to create a look for you. Here, I've made them work five ways — one for every day of the working week. Mix-and-match them to suit your style.

Monday

Top: Wear a striped, puff-sleeved shirt.
Bottom: Try the pencil skirt with a belt, black 40-denier tights and platform courts.
Coat: Go for the mac.
Accessories: Stud earrings, watch and a bag.

Tuesday

Top: Wear a jacket (with a vest underneath).
Bottom: Go for black, straight-leg or high-waisted trousers or jeans and platform courts.
Coat: You've got the jacket on, but wear the mac, too, if you like.
Accessories: Bold necklace — though nothing too fussy — or a pair of simple gold or silver earrings and a bag.

RIGHT Organizer and pen, Louis Vuitton.

Wednesday

Top: Go for a shirtdress and button it down to just above the bust. Roll the sleeves up. Remove the belt it came with and tie a tan belt around your waist instead.

Bottom: Try black 40-denier tights in winter, or bare, tanned legs in summer; tan courts.

Coat: Wear the jacket with the sleeves pushed up to elbows, or go jacket-free in summer.

Accessories: Big, black, chunky bracelet, or gold hoops and a bag.

Thursday

Top: Wear the waistcoat over a shirt, which should be buttoned down to just above where the waistcoat buttons stop.

Bottom: Go for high-waisted trousers; tan courts.

Coat: Try wearing the mac with the sleeves pushed up.

Accessories: Big shades and a tan handbag.

Friday

Top: Choose the waistcoat and wear it with a vest or a T-shirt underneath.

Bottom: Go for straight trousers or skinny black jeans and courts.

Coat: A jacket will work well.

Accessories: Big, chunky bracelets or a big, brightly coloured scarf — or try both.

Real Beauty Note

I think the best make-up look for work is a groomed one, so I'd pull my hair back into a sleek ponytail, make sure my skin was nice and clean and add a little bit of gloss to my lips. I might also sweep some bronzer over my cheeks, forehead and temple area for a natural-looking glow. I don't wear mascara much, but make-up artists say that brown, as opposed to black, can look softer during the day.

IN MY BAG:

- I've always got my phone with me.

- **My diary:** I've had this Louis Vuitton diary for years – I like the way the pages are set out as I need week-to-view so that I don't miss any appointments.

- **My pen:** My mum bought me a silver pen to match my diary.

- **Lip gloss:** I don't go anywhere without it.

- **Flat shoes:** I love my Lanvin ballet flats for when I need some light relief from my heels. Topshop does some great little slip-ons that pack so flat you can easily fit them into a clutch.

RIGHT Mac, Joseph; bag, Warehouse; jeans, J Brand.

Office-to-party

If you're going straight out after work, all you have to do is take a few key accessories with you and you'll have a night-time look in an instant. Here's how I'd make my day-to-night outfits work.

HEELS

Remember to pop a pair of heels in your bag for slipping into at night. Metallic finishes add extra glam-factor.

SKINNY JEANS

The minute you pair a sparkly top with your skinnies, you've got a great night-time look.

BELT

Take a jewelled-buckle belt with you to dress up your top half. Bold belts always add a glam touch to office outfits.

BOLD EARRINGS

I'm not one for wearing big earrings during the day, but at night I love them, as they automatically change my look.

SCARF

At night, wear a big pashmina-style or printed scarf over a blouse: it will add an elegant, evening feel.

GIANT CLUTCH BAG

The clutch is now the 'it-bag' for day, and as soon as you slip on heels at night, it easily fits into night-time mode.

HAIR

I always try to do something different with my hair when I'm going out. Just loosen yours up a bit for an 'undone' look.

MAKE-UP

A couple of sweeps of mascara on the outer lashes adds a hint of sultry glamour to eyes.

Shrug, vintage; sandals, Marlene Birger; bangles, Forever 21, New York.

summer

Summer

When summer arrives, colours get brighter and fabrics feel light and fresh.

Summer is my favourite time of year; but then we're all happier when the sun comes out. Maybe fashion-lovers are even more so, though, as this is when the new spring/summer collections start to appear in the shops, whether in designer boutiques or high-street stores.

I do sometimes find that the shift from a winter to a summer wardrobe can take some getting used to, though. Styles and colours change quite a lot, and after months of covering up in heavier layers, it's time to strip away woolly clothes and put more of our bodies on show. I don't know about you, but I always find that moment a bit tricky.

So that's where this chapter comes in. Here, I'm going to give you some tips on how to adapt your winter wardrobe for warmer weather, including which key pieces you need to stock up on, how to find colours to suit you and how to work some of the major looks that come around every summer into your own style.

 PREVIOUS PAGE Dress, Gucci.

 RIGHT Blouse, vintage; corsage, Johnny Loves Rosie.

Great Summer Basics

VESTS

I'd say it's a good idea to ditch any vests, T-shirts and cotton camis that you've got kicking about from last summer, as they tend to look a bit washed out second time around. Buy a set of crisp, new vests – you can pick these up really cheaply now. A few white tees will always come in handy and you can style up a white tank vest with absolutely anything, while cami tops are great for wearing underneath sheer fabrics. Find vests at: Topshop, Marks & Spencer, Gap, Primark, See by Chloé and Joseph.

Summer style note: buy a few white tanks, so that you can be sure that the one you are wearing is white as can be.

T-SHIRTS

Layered T-shirts are a great summer look, so I like to buy different colours in varying lengths to wear together. I'd also invest in a few good-quality T-shirts as they look smarter and keep their shape longer. Choose from fine-knit V-neck or off-the-shoulder styles in stripy, silky and printed fabrics. Looser shapes have a more designer feel, especially when worn casually tucked into skirts, shorts or cigarette pants (cropped jeans that taper in to just above the ankle). Find T-shirts at: Topshop Unique, Reiss, Jigsaw, Gap and American Apparel.

Summer style note: layer whites and soft, pretty colours.

RIGHT Dress, Freemans.

BLOUSES

The arrival of summer means it's time to leave structured styles behind and go for looser shirts and blouses. Chloé always do this kind of look and I like the fact that it's a little hippyish but modern with it. I'd go for looser or puff-sleeved blouses in soft or sheer cotton. Embroidered white stitching – or broderie anglaise – always looks summery in that lovely Seventies way. Loose, silky, printed tops or floaty chiffon floral styles are also dressy at night. Find blouses at: Ted Baker, Karen Millen, River Island, Next, Warehouse and Kate Moss Topshop.

Summer style note: layer soft, light blouses over vests. Metallic accessories add extra style.

DRESSES

Full-length or maxi-dresses look gorgeous on hot summer days. Roman sandals look great with long dresses, and wedges or espadrilles look good if you like an extra lift. The other style I love for summer is a short, Sixties-style shift. As long as it's not too short it will look quite cool – but I'd always wear this style with flats or thong sandals, as heels can make short hemlines look a bit too sexy for day.

Shirtdresses are good for most figures, though – layer a fine vest underneath yours. Prom-style dresses can be dressed down for day with ballet pumps or plimsolls and a cotton cardi. Find dresses at: Warehouse, Oasis, Topshop, Dorothy Perkins, Reiss, Matches, Net-a-porter, Urban Outfitters, Jaeger, UniQlo and Kate Moss Topshop.

Summer style note: if you're not naturally dark, use some tinted body lotion or fake tan to build a nice glow on your legs, as tights feel horrible in summer and white legs are a 'no-no'. Try Rimmel Sunshimmer. It's instant, non-streaky and washes off with soap and water.

Dress, Pinko; necklace, Sport Max.

BOTTOMS

Some jeans can feel too heavy for hot weather, so try thinner three-quarter-length styles – Topshop always do them. Wide-leg trousers can look quite polished, and sailor-style ones with a high waist and buttons can look really cute with a fine-knit top tucked in. Capri pants – knee-length tapered styles – are a good option, while denim cut-offs and shorts can look good dressed up with a white shirt. Other shorts to choose include tailored city shorts that are cut just above the knee. Find shorts at: Topshop, Gap, Urban Outfitters, French Connection, Jigsaw, Debenhams and George at Asda.

Summer style note: slim-leg shorts that stop just above the knee are good for curvy figures. Be careful of any trouser or shorts with pleating around the waistline, though, as they can look frumpy. Wedges and ballet flats look great with shorts.

SKIRTS

Most of us can get away with wearing minis with thick black tights in winter, but too much flesh on show in summer can be a disaster. Denim pencil skirts are a good alternative to minis, and cotton tulip or bubble skirts, which come a bit higher up the knee, are also smart. Dirndl skirts – those wider, sticky-out styles – are really summery. Look for ones in plain white or pretty colour combinations. Find skirts at: Miss Selfridge, Oasis, Warehouse, H&M, Reiss, French Connection, Topshop, Net-a-porter, ASOS.

Summer style note: balance out wide skirt shapes with a vest or blouse. Narrow skirt styles look nice with a big-sleeved blouse.

JACKETS

Sometimes a cardi is the only cover-up you need in summer, but for breezier days, try a blazer-style jacket or a cotton bomber. Both will look good with trousers or skirts and dresses. If you like a sporty look, pick up a super-light parka for a hip, casual look. Find jackets at: Gap, River Island, Miss Selfridge, UniQlo, American Apparel, French Connection, Joseph and Kate Moss at Topshop.

Summer style note: go for jackets in lighter fabrics and colours, like stone or pale grey, as they will work with most summer clothes.

❀ SHORT CUT

Jacket, Joseph; shoes, LK Bennett; necklace, Sport Max.

Classic summer looks

BOHO

The Bohemian look is one that I just instantly associate with summer. Designers change their take on this look every year, so there's always a new twist to it, but Boho-chic is always about being soft, loose and casually feminine. I think maxi-dresses fall well into the Boho trend; they always seem to come in nice colourful or printed fabrics and look ultra-feminine when dressed up with accessories. Clashing patterns and embroidered fabrics are classic Boho touches.

How to do Boho now: there's a real Seventies feel to the Boho look now, so go for a wide-sleeved or loose blouse in a floral print, and wear it with high-waisted jeans and some brown leather wedges (brown accessories are good with Boho looks as black can look too harsh). A long, white dress tied at the waist with a big tan belt and worn with some high, square-heeled brown or tan boots is a look I like. I've seen Kylie wear an outfit like this, and she looked great in it. Bold gold or silver earrings and necklaces will add a sexy touch. Leather open-toe sandals or wedges and a Seventies-style saddlebag are the perfect finishing touches.

FESTIVAL CHIC

This is a look that Alexa Chung and Agyness Deyn look so cool in. It's a bit of a mix-and-match style – like jeans with a blazer or waistcoat – and it really comes down to how you put different styles together. Try wearing a blazer over a floaty floral dress.

How to do Festival chic now: a mix of prettier styles with a bit of simple sportswear thrown in is a new way of doing the festival look.

Try wearing a strapless floral dress with a T-shirt underneath and some plimsolls. Or, wear high-waisted jeans with a simple grey tank vest and loads of necklaces. If you live in your skinnies, try layering: go for a long, skinny T-shirt, and wear a short tuxedo jacket over it. You might also pick a pretty tea dress and rough it up a little by topping it with a loose leather jacket and scarf. Go for strappy platforms or short biker boots here, or just keep it plain and simple with a big, flouncy, ruffle blouse and some denim shorts and espadrilles.

WHITE

Because it is the shade of summer, if you go for white you can't really fail: whether you like a sleek look – like a white, tailored jacket with jeans, or a full skirt with a T-shirt – you'll always find some nice white pieces that you'll wear all summer long.

How to do white now: the key with white is to keep it as simple as possible. I'd probably go for a long, cotton, maxi dress or a little structured sundress that fits closely around the waist and bust but comes out at the hips. Anything with ruffles or crochet details will look nice. Or, if you want something a little more glamorous, draped goddess style dresses look great, too. If you prefer a dressed-down look, choose simple T-shirt dresses in heavier, looser fabrics, and sling on a gold or brown hipster belt. And for a really chic take, add a splash of bold colour: lift white capri pants and a white blouse with a bright yellow bag, or a lilac scarf, for instance. Or stack some gold bracelets or neck-laces – gold jewellery always looks beautiful against white.

 ABOVE LEFT Bracelets, Freedom at Topshop.

 T-shirt, Topman.

Shorts

We can't avoid them in summer as they are all over the shops, and in winter they can look great with thick black tights, but knowing which shorts suit your shape in summer can be tricky. So, here's a little advice on wearing shorts.

If you've got a curvy figure...

If your waist is your best bit, go for straight-cut shorts or ones that sit close to the leg – like cut-off skinny jeans, or capri styles. A slim, tailored, city-short look can work well, but if you're worried about your bum or your thighs, cover them with a nice big shirt pulled in at the waist with a belt. If your tummy's a problem area, go for plain, flat-fronted shorts without pockets. Regardless of your body shape, wear shorts with some great wedges and your legs will look twice as long.

If you've got a slim figure...

If you're slim you can go for more casual styles that are cut quite high on the thigh. Ballet pumps and flat sandals look great worn with shorts on long, slim legs, and heels can lengthen shorter legs. Looser styles can balance out really well with a flared top and some mid-height espadrilles. Find summer shorts at: Gap, American Apparel, French Connection, Warehouse, Hennes, Primark, Topshop, Stella McCartney and Juicy Couture.

Switch to summer colour

If you're dark or olive skinned… this is your time of year to shine. Blocks of bright colours, like orange, yellow and pink, will look fantastic on you, and you should try experimenting with bolder looks – like a bright yellow top and a pristine white skirt. Pastels will also look nice, but bright colours are best.

If you're fair skinned… classic shades like white, red and navy can work in summer, but bright ones will clash with your skin tone, while pastels (like powder-pink, pale blue and lemon) could really wash you out. Black is too harsh and might make paler skins look sickly, but bold patterns and prints are a good choice for you in summer. And, if you top up your fake tan regularly, a healthy glow will make these colours look nicer against your skin. Remember, if you have fair skin, wear longer sleeves over vests and cami tops to protect it from the sun.

Designers change their take on the Boho look all the time, but clashing colours are a key element.

❀ Top, ASOS.

Summer nights

Sometimes all you need are a few little extras in order to change your look as you move from lazy days to balmy nights. Here are a few options:

1 You'll make good use of a cardigan all summer, so it's worth investing in a decent one in a colour that goes with everything. Spend a little more and it will last you through the summer.

2 A brightly coloured, big scarf is great for tying loosely round your neck in early evening and also for using as a shawl later in the night.

3 Bold bracelets and big arm cuffs dress up summer daywear perfectly. Just add a white dress and some gold thong sandals for a simply gorgeous outfit.

4 Throw a tiered, chiffon floral blouse, or a pretty single-colour silk T-shirt over a pair of three-quarter length trousers for a touch of night-time style. Metallic high-heel sandals will look good if you're going clubbing.

5 Whether it's a loose, T-shirt style in cotton, or a smarter chiffon style, a draped dress can be so easily dressed up with a pair of fabulous shoes and a sleek hairdo. Wear hair up if it's long, smooth it down a little if it's short, and accent waves if it's curly. Some gold bracelets will finish off the outfit nicely.

6 A graphic printed tunic with big flowers, say or sections of bright colour will dress up nicely for night with a shimmery evening bag. Dare to bare your legs if you have a sunkissed glow, or for a hint of colour try Lancome's Flash Bronzer Self-tanning Leg Gel. Flat sandals or wedges will look good, too.

Dress, Warehouse; shoes, Jimmy Choo; bangle, Topshop.

gymwear

Gymwear

From clothing to trainers, here are my tips for getting your fitness wear into gear.

Gym classes were never really my favourites at school; the only team I was in was rounders, so maybe that's why I was never too fussed about my gym kit.

When I was younger I went to dance school. Then a few years ago I started going to the gym. When the idea of doing my first fitness DVD came up, I was keen to take on the challenge but it wasn't just my body that got a workout then – my kit needed to look a whole lot fitter, too.

I have continued working out with my trainer Elise and I try to do three sessions a week. I'm not one for posing on the treadmill – the thought of that makes me fold up laughing – but I do put a lot more thought into my fitness routine now, and also what I wear when exercising. That's not just because I want to wear stuff that looks good, but because proper sports clothes can make you feel a whole lot more comfortable during your session. So there are a few valid reasons for getting some proper kit for exercising, and wanting to look good is just one of them.

In this chapter I'm going to show you how to put together a working fitness kit and will advise you on some of the things you should look out for when buying exercise gear – from clothing to trainers. I'll also share a few of the healthy eating and fitness tips I've picked up from the professionals I've worked with. I hope they, and the idea of getting some stylish new kit, help get you motivated too.

PREVIOUS PAGE Tracksuit, Juicy Couture.

You are looking more toned
every time I see you!
(remember to hide a bar
of chocolate in the
sweatyBetty
sweatyBetty

The ultimate fit kit

There are loads of great styles and fabrics to choose from now, and gymwear looks better than ever. Here are my top tips for creating a good-looking, practical gym style.

LAYER UP

Think in terms of layers when deciding what to wear on your top half, so that you can peel them off as you get warmer. Vests and tanks are great because they are not bulky and they cling to your body, almost like a second skin; while most have an in-built mesh band around the bust for extra support. Reebok and Nike do some really nice, plain ones, and Stella McCartney for Adidas ones are a good, structured fit.

If you don't like vests, there's a huge range of short- and long-sleeved sports tops available, and many have fashionable touches, like prints and feminine necklines, or bands of colour that add shape to your figure. It's not all cropped tops, either; you can get longer, more flattering lengths these days, too. Try USA Pro, Nike and Deha at Sweaty Betty.

Once you've got your base-layer sorted, get a comfy hoodie or zip-up sweatshirt to wear on top. This will keep you warm before your session starts and do the same while you cool down again at the end. Nike, USA Pro and Gap Body have some good ones, or try a loose yoga tunic from Stella McCartney for Adidas. American Apparel also does vests in brilliant colours.

Top, Republic.

Buy your gymgear in a nice, bright colour: it will give you a boost and help kick-start your routine.

THE BOTTOM LINE

Though choosing gym trousers might depend on the activity you're doing, for me it comes down to the style I feel most comfortable in. I buy a lot of stuff from Nike as it fits my shape – and my legs. So, if you find a brand that works well with your shape, that's half the battle. I love the yoga-style pants that are quite tight at the top and wider at the bottom. Gap now do them with the fold-over waistband, and Sweaty Betty's got a good range of these styles, too. (Another bonus of these trousers is that they really hold you in around the tummy!)

If you like short trousers, I think the most flattering ones are the capri styles that stop on the knee. There are a lot of three-quarter-length or cropped styles out there, but when you pair them with bulky trainers they can make even the longest legs look short. So these are definitely a no-no for me! Try Sheactive for good capri styles. They do a range of plus-size styles, too.

If you prefer the freedom of shorts, you can always wear them over leggings in winter for that New York-style jogger look. Nike does a good range, and Stella McCartney for Adidas does a super-stylish loose pair. American Apparel does a range of tightly fitted ones that are good for summer. Watch out for boxer-short styles or ones with drawstring waists, though, because they can look unflattering around the tummy area.

I love yoga-style pants for working out in: they give good extra support at the waist.

OUT AND ABOUT

If you're training or running outside, it's a good idea to layer up. Light tops with long sleeves are ideal as you can tie them around your waist as you get warmer. Many running and outdoor sports jackets are windproof, but if you train outdoors a lot, it's worth checking that your jacket's waterproof, too. Nike's Tech Clima-FIT jackets are smart, weatherproof and reflective. It's also always worth looking for waterproof stuff in outdoor specialists like Blacks. Stella McCartney for Adidas does some windproof jackets that also protect against light showers.

If you're out pounding the pavements at night, get some reflective gear, or try LED accessories. Nathan does a range that transmits light while you run; their LED arm and ankle straps cost just £14 at Sheactive. A word of caution: if you are running in the dark, remember to steer clear of parks and quiet roads and stick to areas where there are people walking about or cars passing by.

FOOT NOTE

I know it's always tempting to go for what looks best, but the style factor should always come second when it comes to buying trainers. For working out you really need them to protect your joints, especially if you're doing a lot of high-impact aerobics classes. Cross-trainers are good all-rounders, but talk to the footwear specialist in your local sports shop and get advice on shoes for the activities that you do most often. You can expect to pay anything from around £60 for a decent pair. Run and Become, the running shoe specialist, has some great tips for running shoes on its website – which is listed in the Real Style File at the back of this book.

Trainers, Nike.

INSIDE OUT

A good sports bra is crucial when you're working out: like trainers, it's all about support. Most lingerie departments have a section for sports bras, so you can easily pick one up when you are out shopping. If you have time, ask for a proper fitting, just like you would for a normal bra.

If you do high-impact workouts, go for a bra that will really make you feel strapped in; if you've got a smaller bust, a reinforced vest should be fine, but regular bra shapes work best for fuller busts. Shock Absorber bras are some of the best available. Choose a bra that best suits the workout you will be doing – they come in low-, medium- and high-impact versions. Sheactive have split their products into easy-to-find sections, so it's worth checking out their website.

And, while you're at it, get some sports knickers. Everyone tends to forget about these, but most of them have stay-dry technology and they hold you in well, so you'll really feel as though the sit-ups are doing the job. Try Figleaves and Sheactive for nice ranges.

CARRIED AWAY

If you're going to the gym regularly, it's worth getting a smart bag to put your kit in. Something with a waterproof lining is good, as you may have to sling your towel or swimsuit in it, but for style factor, try American Apparel – they have a great selection of designs and colours that won't cost the earth. If you like a designer look, Gucci do a nice cream and black nylon bag that's not too pricey. All the main sports brands have rucksacks and other types of bags to suit you, but I prefer something with more style about it: after all, you'll be carrying it about like any other bag.

Real Gym Note

Some handy peices to keep in your gym bag:

- Travel-size shampoo, conditioner and body wash
- E45 cream for face and body
- Handy-sized hair serum or finishing product
- Padlock and coins for your locker
- Comb
- Water bottle
- Knickers
- Socks
- Tinted lipsalve
- Tinted moisturizer
- Mascara
- Deodorant

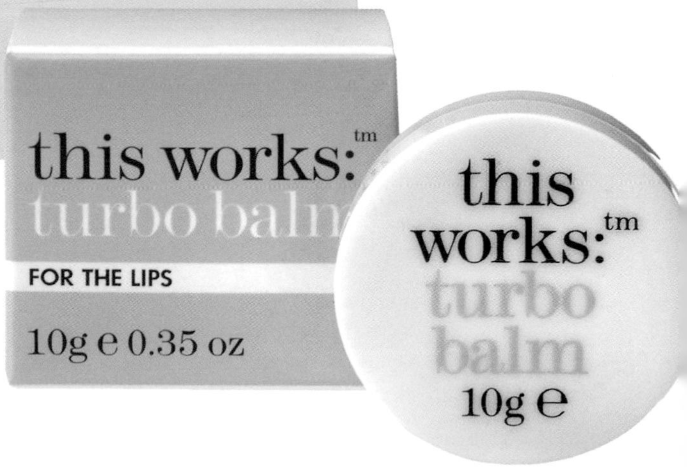

this works:™
turbo balm
FOR THE LIPS
10g e 0.35 oz

this works:™
turbo balm
10g e

My fitness diary

Now that I'm doing more shoots and launches, it makes sense that I look after my body as best I can. Plus, since doing my fitness video I've become good friends with Elise Lindsay, the personal trainer who worked on it with me, and I work out with her every week. Sometimes, if I'm in London or on the move, it's hard to keep up with these regular sessions, but when I get back home I make sure that I get right into it again.

Our session consists of cardio training, such as running outside for 40 minutes, then we'll come back and do squats and lunges, free weights and a good set of stomach and core stuff, like Pilates. To achieve a flat stomach I'd have to work really, really hard and do my sit-ups every day for a good while, though. And so far I've not managed to be that dedicated!

After I've been training for a while I do see a big difference in my legs, and even though it might not seem like I've lost loads of weight, they are more toned and lean. My bum is perkier, too, so I feel much better in jeans.

Going to the gym gets me up and ready for the rest of the day. And there's no doubt that when I'm exercising regularly my posture is much better and I've got a lot more energy.

My food diary

I have a bowl of cereal and some fruit every day. My trainer got me into having breakfast. She said you should always eat something before going to the gym because it gets your metabolism going, and if you go training on an empty stomach, your body's got nothing to work from; whereas when you eat, your body's working with that food straight away. I always leave some time between when I eat and train, though, as it's not good to exercise on a full stomach.

I am careful about what I eat, though I don't think that people should diet their whole lives. I do still go to Weight Watchers occasionally. Now, though, I only go when I think I need to lose a few pounds, and I stick to my diet by myself after that. Like most people, I love my food so I prefer the gradual approach where you can have most things but you've just got to watch the amounts. We often go out for a Chinese, and I can have a really nice dinner just by choosing healthier options, like sea bass and spring onions and noodles. I love dim sum and all the starters like spring rolls, but they are strictly treats.

The bottom line for me is that I love clothes and so I want to be able to feel my best in them – and that's why I am motivated to look after my body as best as I can. And, let's face it, nothing makes you feel better than pulling on your favourite jeans and zipping them up with ease.

I do keep an eye on what I eat but I love my food, so I like my treats, too.

travel

Travel

What to wear when you're travelling and how to look good when you get to your destination.

One of the things I love about going on holiday is getting the chance to wear light, summery styles every day. I must say that I've not got into going skiing or the idea of holidaying in colder countries yet, so I'm just going to stick to talking about clothes for summer holidays in this chapter.

I'm into a hippyish Seventies look for holidays at the moment: that laidback, easy-going style of a printed maxi or kaftan dress worn with a pair of giant sunglasses and some flat sandals. That's one of the best things about dressing for holidays – you can really push the boat out and try different styles.

Whether you're heading off to Ibiza on a girly holiday with your mates or flying off to an exotic destination with your other half, this chapter is all about travelling in style: from what to take on the plane with you, to how to make your wardrobe work.

PREVIOUS PAGE Dress, Moschino; sandals, Gap; bracelets, vintage.

READY TO WEAR

Dress, Pinko; belt, Pinko; sandals, Gap; bangles, Topshop.

Holiday essentials

From suitcase to sunglasses, no matter where I'm going – or how far – there are some travel essentials that I would never be without:

1 A smart suitcase

I understand why some people like to throw their holiday stuff into any old bag – after all, holidays are about chilling out – but for me, nice luggage is a must. There's nothing like a smart suitcase to get any holiday off to a stylish start: and it doesn't have to be expensive.

I think if you're going long-haul, structured cases are nicest, as they always look neat and they often have pockets and zips inside, which are good for separating your wardrobe as you pack. But if you're just off for a weekend, you can choose from some really nice, casual bags now – everyone from Zara to Topshop do them. I'd always recommend choosing a case with wheels, though, because if like me you find it hard to pack light, you'll save yourself having to lug a heavy bag around. You can get fantastic-looking luggage for really good prices on the high street: Marks & Spencer's Leather Collection is gorgeous – especially in white – and TK Maxx has usually got some great designer holdalls and suitcases in. Find smart suitacases at: Tripp at Debenhams, Mandarina Duck at John Lewis, Marks & Spencer and Zara for weekend bags.

SUNNY DELIGHT

Top, Joseph; pumps, Primark; skirt, Reiss; scarf, Reiss; shopper, Primark.

2 Stylish swimwear

My first thought when planning a holiday is 'time for a new bikini'; then straight after that I think: 'time to fit in a few exercise sessions'. I'll never have the perfect figure for the beach, but a few exercise sessions definitely make my legs, bum and tum feel a lot less wobbly. And that means I feel good when I put my new bikini on.

I much prefer wearing a bikini to a swimsuit, but if you're not sure, see the following pages for some tips to help you decide. I've found some really nice bikinis in Warehouse, and I also love Missoni swimwear, which you can pick up in department stores like Selfridges and Harvey Nichols. The Missoni stuff really suits my shape, so I tend to get a new bikini by them every year. It's always worth checking out the swimwear sections in department stores: you'll always find some nice, good-quality, different designs. Find stylist swimwear at: Topshop and Oasis have 'holiday shops' now, where you can buy most things you'll need for going away. Also try Marks & Spencer's Limited Collection and Melissa Odabash at Figleaves.

Bikini, Melissa Odabash.

My top swimwear tips:

- White swimwear looks gorgeous but it can get stained with SPF cream, so if you want to go for white, it's a good idea to pick up a less pricey swimsuit or bikini. And a word of warning – some white swimwear goes see-through when wet!

- If you've got a fuller bust, spend a little more on structured swimwear, as this will support you and define your shape well. Freya does some lovely bikinis and swimsuits.

- If you've got a smaller bust, go for bikinis with textured detail, like ruffles. Bandeau tops also look great on your shape. The Vitamin A range at Figleaves is fantastic.

- If you'd like a swimsuit that holds you in around the tummy and hips, go for a Miraclesuit, which will pull you in at all the right places. Freemans stock these.

- If you're particularly worried about your tummy, get a swimsuit that has a control panel and that plunges at the neckline. And if you prefer a bikini, pick a fuller-brief style.

- Treat your bikini top like you would a bra – if you want to enhance your shape, get an underwired top. But be careful not to get a top that's too small, as it won't look great if everything spills out. Try Panache at Bravissimo. Marks & Spencer have a great range, too.

- If you don't like the idea of a swimsuit but feel that a bikini's not right either – try a tankini: it's like a vest top and shorts. Figleaves and Marks & Spencer do them.

3 Sunglasses

There's nothing cooler than a super-smart pair of sunnies to wear throughout your hols. I have to admit that I always treat myself to a pair of new designer shades when I'm going away, because I know I'm going to get lots of wear out of them and they always make you look a bit smarter in the sun. The lenses are better quality, too, and so I feel like my eyes will be well protected.

Duty-free shopping areas are a good place to pick up sunglasses, as they have all the top brands and their prices are more reasonable than most shops. I always take a couple of high-street pairs with me too, as everyday sunglasses can get in a right mess – being stuffed into your bag or trampled on by the pool. I always make sure that the lenses have UV protection, though. I love big shades just now, like the ones by Pucci or DVB. Find sunglasses at: Linda Farrow Vintage at Harrods, Harvey Nichols, Sunglass Hut at airports, Topshop, Hennes, Next, Marks & Spencer and George at Asda.

What looks cooler than a pair of super-smart sunglasses?

✿ Sunglasses, Linda Farrow Vintage.

4 T-shirt dress

A loose, light cotton T-shirt dress is a great cover-up on holiday, as it will fit easily into your beach bag. I'd say T-shirt dresses suit most shapes and sizes, and you can go as short or as long as you like. Also, it can be easily pulled over your swimsuit or bikini when you want to leave the pool or the beach for a drink.

T-shirt dresses can also be easily glammed up for evening: just slick back your hair and put on a pair of dangly gold earrings and you've got a look. You can get really nice T-shirt dress styles on the high street now. Shops like Oasis and Topshop have great in-store 'holiday' shops , so you can pick them up there. Where to find them: Next, Mango, Accessorize, American Apparel.

Necklace, Pilgrim; dress, American Apparel; scarf, Accessorize.

5 Simple footwear

You definitely need an everyday flat shoe with good comfort factor when you go on your hols – rubber-soled Havaiana flip-flops are just the easiest things to live in when you're on holiday, so I'd always throw a pair of these into my suitcase. Some of the pretty coloured Birkenstock sandals are nice, but I'd stick to wearing these kinds of shoes by the pool or on the beach, as they can look a bit dowdy and too casual at night. I'd also steer clear of Crocs, as I think that they can look really unflattering. Roman sandals are a great suits-all choice.

Oh, and remember to book in for a pedicure before you go on holiday – it will make you feel lovely and groomed the whole time. Where to find holiday shoes: (flip flops) Havaianas and Birkenstocks at Office, Uniqlo. (Roman sandals) Office, Topshop, Net-a-Porter, Matches and Nine West.

In-flight checklist

Being organized makes any journey a whole lot easier and far less stressful. So I always make sure that I've got everything I will need on the plane packed into a smart, mid-sized bag. If you like to travel light, buy a stylish beach bag that can double up as your hand luggage. Here's what I carry in mine:

Pashmina or big scarf: you can wear it as a shawl, a scarf or use it as a pillow. I'd never travel without one.

Cashmere socks: they are a great comfort for feet on long-haul journeys and keep you warm in chilly air cabins.

This Works travel kit: this selection of gorgeous travel-size products made from plant oils includes lip balm, eye serum, and moisturizer, and it is perfect for in-flight pampering. It will help keep your skin, lips and eyes in tip-top condition while you're flying.

Giant sunglasses: Not only will they cover up tired eyes after a long flight, but they'll help you to step off the flight looking glamorously fresh.

Bottled water: it's always a good idea to keep hydrated on a long flight: your skin will benefit and you'll feel fresher when you reach your destination, too. Pick one up just before you board as you can't take it through check-in under the current security checks.

Travel wallet: I've got a pink travel wallet that I keep all my travel documents and my passport in – and because it's so bright, it's easy to find in my bag when I need it!

travel

8 miracle products to keep you beautiful from take-off to landing and beyond

thisworks™

Travel kit, This Works.

10 easy travel pieces

Here are 10 things I'd recommend that you pack for going away. You don't have to stick to my choices, but the idea of this list is to prove that a travel-light wardrobe doesn't have to be short on style.

1 SMART TOP: a cotton or a silk blouse will feel cool and soft on warm skin. Go for either a big, loose, see-through one or a fine, silky, short-sleeved one in white or a bold colour. Shop for tops at: Reiss, Topshop, Butterfly by Matthew Williamson at Debenhams, Paul & Joe, French Connection, Chloé, and Biba at Matches.com.

2 THREE-QUARTER-LENGTH TROUSERS: a pair of slim, three-quarter-length, light cotton trousers will go with most things and feel comfortable (some jean styles can be too heavy for wearing when it's hot). Shop for trousers at: Topshop, Juicy Couture, Oasis, Gap, Matches.com and Mango.

3 VEST TOP: I love white tank vests as they look so fresh next to tanned skin and can be easily pepped up with jewellery; perfectly chic for those nights when you don't really feel like dressing up. Shop for vests at: Topshop, Marks & Spencer, Joseph, C&C California at Matches.com.

4 COTTON SHIRT: A cotton broderie-anglaise blouse (this fabric looks like it has little embroidered holes in it) is a fresh way to cover up on long, hot days. Buy it short and cropped or longer and looser with a little neck detail if you prefer to take the focus away from your bum and tum. Shop for them at: Kate Moss Topshop, Next, Chloé and Freemans.

5 SKIRT OR SHORTS: a nice pair of crisp, cotton shorts or a loose skirt with a gathered waistband are both good outfit choices for early-evening drinks. Make sure the waistband isn't too tight, though, as it will feel really uncomfortable in hot weather. Slim short styles are flattering and they come in different lengths (see my shorts guide on page 160 for more tips). Choose a plain white skirt for a really clean look, or a simple, bold print. Shop for skirts and shorts at: La Redoute, Net-a-porter, Topshop, Oasis, Miss Selfridge and Hennes.

6 GRECIAN-STYLE DRESS: I just love the Grecian look – and it really works on suntanned skin. A white one will look gorgeous if you have a nice tan, or go for soft peachy pink or emerald green, depending on what you think suits your skin tone best. See my 'switch to summer colour' section on page 161. Shop for dresses at: Oasis, Topshop, Reiss, 3.1 Philip Lim at Net-a-porter, Joseph and Warehouse.

7 GOLD NECKLACE: Gilt jewellery looks lovely in the sun – it's shiny but not too blingy and will add a touch of elegance to outfits. Go for long pendant styles or a Grecian torque style, but make it a statement piece and it will look gorgeous with all your summer gear – and it means you don't have to weigh your case down with tons of other stuff. Shop for necklaces at: Accessorize, Freedom at Topshop, New Look, Dorothy Perkins and Net-a-Porter.

8 OVERSIZED EARRINGS: Get a pair of gorgeous drop, hoop or jewelled earrings to glam night-time looks up. I think oversized styles look fantastic, but I'd always stick to my accessories rule: don't do statement earrings and necklaces together or else you'll crowd your look. Shop for earrings at: Monet at Stylefinder.com, Freedom at Topshop, Mikey, Zoe, LJBLondon.com, and Erickson Beamon at Debenhams.

9 BELT: A leather belt or any belt with gold or metallic detail will add a classic touch to earrings and necklaces. It will look just as nice looped through your white trousers for day as it will clasped around your Grecian dress at night. Shop for belts at: Freedom at Topshop, Karen Millen, Ted Baker, Accessorize and Roberto Cavalli at Net-a-porter.

10 BAG: A slouchy bag in tan, or one with a metallic finish, will work perfectly from day to night. However, anything too big will look a bit daft at night, so keep it mid-sized. I think Accessorize do some great holiday bags. Or pack a metallic clutch bag for night and just use your beach bag for day. Shop for bags at: Accessorize, Topshop, Russell & Bromley, Next, Net-a-Porter and Brownsfashion.com.

Cuff, Accessorize.

5 day-to-night looks

So now that you've got your holiday wardrobe sorted – including your 10 easy pieces and your essentials – here are some suggestions as to how to mix-and-match them while you're away.

Monday:

Top: white vest or cotton top
Bottom: three-quarter-length trousers
Accessories: gold belt and Roman sandals from your essentials
At night: dress up this outfit with the oversized earrings

Tuesday:

Top: Grecian dress
Bottom: bare legs
Accessories: bag and sandals
At night: add heels and oversized earrings

Wednesday:

Top: kaftan
Bottom: bikini or swimsuit
Accessories: sunglasses, sandals and bag
At night: remove swimsuit or bikini and pull kaftan in at the waist with the belt; add oversized earrings

Thursday:

Top: white vest
Bottom: white skirt or shorts
Accessories: gold necklace, bag and sandals
At night: layer up with the floaty blouse and belt it in at the waist

Friday:

Top: Cotton top
Bottom: three-quarter-length trousers
Accessories: bag and sandals
At night: add the gold necklace

Real Beauty Note

The first thing I always pack in my beauty kit when I go on holiday is some SPF cream. I like a high-protection factor (like 15–20 for day) and I also use an SPF 25 moisturizer on my face. After-sun lotion is a great way to stop skin peeling, so it's always worth taking one. Use a really high-protection sun cream, like 30 or 40, for the first few days, as not only will this stop you burning, it will help you to develop a gradual tan that will last. Single application SPFs are ideal if you don't want to slather on cream every two hours: try Piz Buin 1-Day Long – it's suitable for fair skins, too. A lot of my mates also top up their colour with an everyday tanner, like Johnson's Holiday Skin or St Tropez Everyday. Fake Bake does a handy self-tan travel kit, too.

winter

Winter

Top tips on how to revitalize your wardrobe for great seasonal style.

There's something quite nice about the idea of cosying up for autumn and winter. Not least because it's time to revamp your wardrobe to suit the colder days and darker nights.

Unlike summer, where you seem to change your outfits a lot during the day, winter styles tend to be more long-lasting and, of course, they've got to be practical – which is something that fashion-lovers like me never like to think about. It's the keeping warm side of things that can make winter styles so hard to pull off, especially on really cold days when you feel that all you want to do is wrap yourself up.

But there's also lots to look forward to: lovely knitwear, cool boots, smart coats and the new season's bags are just some of the things we might be thinking about stocking up on. You do have to spend a bit more on some winter styles, as they come in heavier fabrics, but then these pieces also tend to have more staying power, which means you should get wear out of them year after year.

And that's what this chapter is all about: putting together some great practical and stylish pieces on which to base your winter look. Here's how.

PREVIOUS PAGE Mac, Joseph; bag, Warehouse; jeans, J Brand; shoes, Christian Louboutin.

Winter basics

CARDIGANS

When buying knitwear, I'd say go for cardigans – you can wear fine T-shirts underneath them, which gives a nice line at the neck and stops them squaring off your figure too much. Also, you can easily tie a cardigan in at the waist to give you added shape.

A fine knit cardigan is something you'll get loads of wear out of in colder months, too, especially in autumn: it's warm enough to wear over pretty blouses, and wearing one with skirts, smart trousers or jeans will keep you warm but won't bulk you up. Try Topshop and French Connection for chunky knits and Marks & Spencer and Next for finer ones.

Style tip: make your chunky knit the focus of your look by wearing it like a coat, with just a plain T-shirt and leggings underneath. Tie it at the waist with a wide belt, and just add some black knee-high boots, an oversized handbag and some sunglasses. Update your fine-knit cardi by wearing a blouse with some lovely detail around the neckline under it, and cinching it in at the waist with a skinny belt.

🌸 Cardigan, Next.

SWEATER DRESSES

I love wearing sweater dresses in winter: not only are they unbelievably comfortable and warm, but they also give you a ready-made look. That kind of effortless style can be just the thing you need on a cold winter's morning. Go for a clingy style if you want to show off your curves, or try a tunic if you want a little more cover. Gap do some nice sweater dresses.

Style tip: Buy an oversized men's cashmere V-neck (Marks & Spencer and Tesco do them), belt it in at the waist and you've got a mini sweater dress. Wear it with tights and boots. Or update last year's dress by wrapping a big, loose-knit scarf casually around your neck.

WINTER COATS

You're likely to spend more on a winter coat than on any other piece in your wardrobe, so look for a good, all-round, classic style that you think will look just as good with jeans as it will with smarter outfits, as you'll want to get lots of wear out of it. Try belted mac- or military-style designs in autumn.

I quite like wearing capes in autumn, but I also always have a parka-style or padded coat to hand for casual days. Again, I'd go for one with more fit and detail so that I don't look too padded! I used to love Puffa styles, but they can have the effect of making you look like a duvet on legs. I think Burberry and Alexander McQueen do some of the most gorgeous coat shapes every year. Also try Gap, Jigsaw, Jaeger, Whistles, French Connection, Zara and Net-a-porter.

Style tip: changing the buttons on your winter coat from year to year will really freshen it up.

Jacket, Gap.

TROUSERS

Black skinny jeans are great for winter because they always look smart, feel comfy, and tuck nicely into knee-high boots. But if you're fed up wearing skinnies, try the new, wide-leg trousers with wedges or square-heeled round-toe boots instead. And, if in doubt, plain black, narrow-cut trousers – like suit trousers – are easily dressed down or up with a fashiony top and will really go with anything. French Connection, Whistles and Gap are good places to try, or go for some high-waisted trousers in a tweedy fabric and wear them with a polo neck. Wool shorts worn with thick tights and court shoes can look great if you like showing off your legs. Topshop always do a great selection.

Style tip: when winter starts, get all your trousers that you've kept from last year dry-cleaned. They'll come back neatly pressed and they'll look like new. Buy new shoes to update last season's looks – for day, wear skinnies with some brightly coloured ballet pumps, and at night, paint your toes in a gorgeously glam colour and step into a pair of patent peep-toes.

200

RIGHT Boots, Hobbs.

Jeans, Freemans.

BOOTS

In winter, everyone needs a great pair of high-heeled boots as well as a good flat pair. I think flat ones are worth spending a bit more on as they really see some wear and tear. I always try to pick up styles with even a tiny bit of a heel, as I'm just not a fan of total flats. I love square-heel boots and round-toe styles, as they go well with skirts, dresses and trousers. For day, I might wear my black Uggs – they look okay with a sweater dress or jeans. Knee-high, biker-style or riding boots never date, and these can all be worn with jeans or skirts and dresses. My mate got a great pair of knee-high biker boots from Tesco last winter. Kurt Geiger and Russell & Bromley also do stylish selections of practical boot styles every year, and Marks & Spencer always do an OK pair.

Style tip: Instead of going straight for black, try dark brown or soft grey leather to add a different edge to your style. You can always get leather dye and dye light-coloured summer boots a darker, wintry colour – or ask your local shoe repair shop to do it. Also, think about having a good-quality pair of stiletto ankle boots in your cupboard, as they can look great with bubble skirts and jeans and are dressy enough for parties.

Knee-high, biker-style or riding boots never date, and these can all be worn with jeans or skirts and dresses.

PARTY DRESS

Everyone needs a do-all, glam cocktail dress that will suit all the different events that you get invited to throughout the festive season: whether it's a work drinks party or a Christmas Eve dinner. Shapes that don't really date are body-skimming shifts like the dresses that Roland Mouret designs; sleeveless styles – they look particularly nice on winter nights because the bare skin across the shoulders and neck looks elegant; Sixties shifts with jewelled or sequined detail; and Fifties-style prom dresses.

The key to winter party dresses, though, is to look for fabrics like lace, velvet, silk taffeta and chiffon, as the textures are so luxurious and special, making them more dressy. If you're going for black, try looking for something with added detail, like beading or sequins, for a more modern look. Also, it's worth remembering that whereas in summer you might not want to go too short, you can wear dresses with matt tights in winter, so can get away with higher hems.

Style tip: Dress simple styles up with a great pair of shoes and jewellery. If you want a really edgy look, wear brightly coloured tights.

In winter, go for luxurious special fabrics like lace, velvet and silk.

LEFT Bracelet, Pilgrim at Debenhams.

COCKTAIL HOUR

Dress, vintage Moschino; shoes, Moschino; cuff, Topshop.

Classic winter looks

MILITARY

One of the great things about winter dressing is that the heavier fabrics mean that many clothes are more tailored, which means added definition for your figure, too. Military styles fall well into this category, and they work particularly well when it comes to jackets and coats. Choose styles with brass buttons at the front and on the cuffs for a really smart touch. Military-style capes can also look cute with skinnies, or sailor-style pea coats (short, double-breasted wool jackets) are good for pairing with jeans at the week-end. High-waisted trousers with button detail on the waistband can also look super-smart with just a black polo neck; or super-cool with a stripy sweater.

How to do military now: Kate Moss often wears a cropped, military-style jacket over a long T-shirt and just jeans; look out for one in her Topshop collection. Shorter, military-inspired jackets also look great over a bubble-hem or a tulip skirt. A looser army style looks good worn with a big scarf. Long, calf-length trench coats look great belted around the waist or worn loose over a long evening dress.

URBAN

Everyone loves dressing up their jeans in winter, and it's nice to wear them with something other than a jumper when going shopping or meeting your mates for coffee. Urban style combines casual with a bit of rock-chic and the odd smart touch thrown in – a fashiony update of your everyday style, really. Think of choosing leather belts with more metallic detail – like studs or big buckles on them – or sturdy leather handbags with chunky metal fastenings. You might even throw a soft, biker-style leather jacket over a little black dress, for instance, and accessorize with a luxurious wool beanie or scarf. The clothes in Sienna Miller's own fashion label, Twenty8Twelve, have elements of this look. Burberry always has this urban feel to its winter collections.

How to do urban now: If you're wearing jeans on the bottom, tuck them into your boots and layer up on top with long, skinny knits over vests, and throw on a casual leather jacket or bomber. Scarves are great for adding edge (Alexander McQueen does some lovely chiffon ones with printed skulls on), as they bring a light, luxurious touch to heavier fabrics. Also, think about mixing glam with casual, like a classic tux jacket over an evening gown, or jeans with a smart chiffon top. A satin pencil skirt can look fantastic with a chunky-knit cardi. Another good urban must-have is a parka-style coat. Go for ones with luxury details, like a big, soft fake-fur collar, or a more feminine, shapely cut.

BEATNIK

I love this look, which is very French and the kind of thing that Brigitte Bardot used to wear. It's more of an autumn than a winter look, but as our winters seem to be getting warmer it could work well into the colder months. The idea is to pair basic shapes together to create a classic, but young, look. A belted mac, a polo neck, some ballet flats and skinny black trousers make up the basic outfit, but you can easily update it.

How to do beatnik now: In winter, think about a navy or a black mac instead of classic beige, as they will complement darker winter colours. Black skinny jeans or tapered trousers will look good on the bottom. Tuck your jeans into knee-high, round-toe leather boots and wear a black-and-white striped sweater. A pencil skirt will work with the sweater, too, when worn with knee-high boots. Add a donkey jacket, a pair of classic sunglasses and an oversize leather bag to complete the look.

 Mac, Principles.

Real Style Note

- Big, bold jewellery can look great with chunky knitwear – whether it's a beaded necklace or chunky stone bracelets. Belts with metal detailing, or patent styles, can also update winter looks. I'd also always have a few different scarves in my wardrobe: a big, square, fine wool one in grey or rich gold will update coats and knitwear; a silk designer or vintage necktie will add style to a plain V-neck sweater; and a long, knitted skinny one can be wrapped around your neck to lift casual looks – go for a really bright colour.

- Tights-wise, sheer ones are always a bit mature-looking, so I'd say always go for high-denier styles: such as 40 or 70. Fishnets can look great with prom styles and knee-length skirts, but they're a definite no-no with minis, in my book.

- And, of course, bags get bigger and better in winter. An oversized shopper will really add to your look in the day, and a gorgeous jewelled or fake-skin clutch will set it off at night. I also love my Reiss sequined beanie to add style to cold winter days.

Earrings, Erickson Beamon at Debenhams.

parties

Parties

Great tips for going out, glamming up and getting ready to party.

I love going out and I love dressing for special occasions. So, whether I'm heading out for a night's dancing with my mates or getting ready for some glamorous event, I always love putting a lot of effort into looking and feeling special.

Sometimes, though, the thought of having to dress up for an occasion can be a bit overwhelming, and knowing what to wear can be a hard call. But I've got a good general rule now: whatever I choose, I wear something because I love it and because I think it looks lovely on me. I'm not one for trying to look too sexy on a night out, and I'm not out to impress anyone: I just love putting on something that makes me feel gorgeous.

I've been lucky enough to be invited to a lot of glamorous events over the past few years – whether it's my mates' weddings or big parties and openings – and that means that I've also learned a lot about the outfits that work for me and the ones that don't. And that's just what I'm going to help you to do, too…

Offset a pretty, girly dress with some killer platform heels.

PREVIOUS PAGE Dress, Lanvin.

Long v short

With so many lovely evening styles to choose from, I often find myself standing in a shop not having any idea what to go for. Luckily for my shopping buddies, I'm much better – and quicker – at working this out now. One way to speed up the process is to think: long or short? Here are my top tips for helping you decide.

Take the long way round

If it's going to be a special occasion it's got to be a special dress, and, for me, nothing makes you feel more glam than a long, floor-skimming number. I just love any chance to wear long dresses. Not only do I feel elegant in them, I like the fact that they can cover everything up in the nicest way. My favourite styles are those with a Grecian feel to them.

Style Tip

When it comes to evening styles, most of us need a little extra help in the underwear department. Control underwear – like Spanx pants, Magic Knickers and control bodies – will pull you in and flatten you out in all the right places, giving your figure a leaner, smoother line. Just don't go for anything too tight.

Shoes, Jimmy Choo.

NEED TO KNOW: TOP TIPS FOR MAXI STYLES

- If you are curvy, go for something that is quite clingy, as this will highlight your curves really well. If you're short, strapless maxi shapes might be a better option.

- If you are pear-shaped, go for a real waist-cinching number that is low-cut at the neck. Grecian styles could work well for you, as they tend to have a band at the waist and the draped fabric will soften the lines around your bottom.

- If you are apple-shaped, a figure-skimming – but not clingy – single-shoulder dress is a nice idea, as it puts all the focus on your upper half. Go for a darker colour, like inky blue or black. Some super-high heels will balance out your figure, too.

- If you are short, don't shy away from wearing long dresses; I used to do this because I thought they would not work on my short frame, but then I found that if I go for one that drapes down from right under the bust line, it makes me look taller and works just fine. Now, I love wearing them.

Dress, Monsoon.

Take a short cut

I love wearing shorter dresses even in winter. Again, my legs aren't the best parts of my body, but sometimes a short dress can make them look longer. (I always add super-high heels anyway.) My favourite styles are Sixties shift dresses, and I quite like ones with prints on them. You can get some lovely silky styles now that look really smart for night, and they're not as formal as long dresses, so they are a good choice for anyone who doesn't like to go for the real grown-up glamour of long styles.

HOW TO DO SHORT ...

- If you are curvy, go for a strapless, clingy number and cinch it in at the waist with a big glam belt. Wear it with platform soles and a blazer-style jacket to make it look edgy.

- If you are pear-shaped, a shift style in a single colour with some embellishment or detail around the neckline would be nice. Wear with high-heeled sandals. Alternatively, a strapless number that's gathered around the bust and that comes in at the waist will balance out your shape.

- If you are apple-shaped, loose, short shifts can look lovely on you as they highlight your legs. If you want to wear something clingier, though, go for a dark-coloured dress with a deep neckline, as this will flatter your shape more. You can always wear a looser shape, too, but clasp it around the hips with a wide belt to give a little more structure.

- If you are short, wear anything that's patterned or printed, as this will draw attention away from your legs. Sleeveless styles are good for this, too. And don't forget to put on the highest heels you can find.

Dress, La Redoute.

Shorter dresses are a good option when you don't want to go for the all-out glamour of a full-length dress but still want to feel special.

215

Classic party looks

JEWELLED

Clothes decorated with sequins, stones and jewels instantly look glamorous, and there are a lot more of them in the shops now. I love dresses with interesting details on them. I had a gorgeous French Connection shift dress that had bands of gold sequins around it, and it was one of those things I could just slip on and feel great in. It took all the hard work out of dressing up, and that's one of the great things about sparkly styles; they just add instant glam. A friend of mine also had a dress with lots of little coins around the neck that was gorgeous. I think Marchesa do great styles like this. Find jewelled styles at: Monsoon, French Connection, Net-a-porter, Oasis, Chloé, Alice Temperley, Mango and Warehouse.

How to do jewelled now: All the high-street stores do dresses and tops with nice beading on them now. Dress these pieces up by boosting the glam factor with your own sparkly jewellery and high, high heels. Or, if you don't feel comfortable getting really dressed up, a beaded top or vest will look gorgeous with some skinny black trousers and some classic stilettos.

Fur tippet and dress, vintage; shoes, Jimmy Choo.

NIGHT BRIGHTS

You should always have a safe evening option hanging in your wardrobe, and the mags always talk about 'the little black dress', but I think it's nice to do something different now and again. That's not to say that I won't wear black, but if I do, I prefer black pieces with texture, like ruffles around the hem or jet stones, to make them a bit more interesting.

I think a more modern thing to do is to wear a dress in a super-bright colour, like a fuchsia-pink satin shift or midnight-blue silk strapless number. Wearing block bold colours is a real trend at big red-carpet dos, like the Oscars or the Brits now. Cheryl Cole looked fantastic in a bright yellow dress with a little gold belt at the Brits this year. And that's one of the reasons that I love Lanvin dresses: the bold colours, luxurious fabrics and beautifully fitted styles are ultra-chic and feminine. Find night brights at: Marks & Spencer's Limited Collection, New Look, Topshop, Mango, Miss Selfridge, 3.1 Philip Lim at Net-a-porter and Wallis.

How to do night brights now: Full-on colour can be quite hard to carry off, and I wonder if that's why people often stick to black? Don't be put off, though, once you find shades that suit your skin tone you'll probably get so into colour that you'll feel dowdy going back to black again. If you're dark or olive-skinned, turquoise or the really bright citrusy shades, such as orange or yellow, will look striking on you. If you're pale, try rich blues and deep reds or purple; or think about bold, bright prints instead.

Classic styles in super-bright colours are a hip and modern alternative to the little black dress.

Dress, Matthew Williamson; shoes, Christian Louboutin.

DRESSED-UP DRESSING DOWN

This trend might sound a bit odd but it's great for those times when you don't want to dress in such a full-on, red-carpet kind of way. Sometimes, if you are just going to a club or a drinks party, turning up in a full-length number might make you look and feel a tad too over-dressed.

And some people prefer a low-key kind of glam anyway; a lot of people do this by wearing trouser suits, but I think they can look a bit mature. What is quite nice, though, is what a friend of mine sometimes does – she'll wear a tuxedo-style jacket over a glittery shift dress and carry a simple clutch bag – like a fake snakeskin one. A tux jacket – which, with its satin lapels, is quite glam anyway – can also look great over a long dress. Kate Moss does this look really well. Find dressed-up dressing down styles at: Kate Moss Topshop, Hennes, Paul & Joe and Next.

How to do dressed-up, dressing down now: The key is to add something quite simple or daywear-style to a really glitzy dress; or pair a really glam top with a pair of classic trousers or jeans (though I'd stick to black and really dark denim for evenings as they look much smarter). You can do a lot with accessories, such as add a plain tan belt to a sheeny dress or a shiny, big gold belt to a plain dress. A really glittery top can look brilliant with some skinny black jeans: just add big earrings and a clutch and you'll shine the whole night through.

Every girl should have a classic black tuxedo in her wardrobe.

 Clutch, River Island.

 RIGHT Jacket, Emporio Armani; brooch, Coast.

Real Style Note

Accessories are a huge part of dressing up, and I covered them in more detail earlier (pages 100–129). In general, though, I think these pieces will always add an extra-special touch:

• A small evening bag or clutch in a luxury or metallic fabric

• High heels: they are a must for night-time styles. Flats are too casual, though jewelled sandals can look great for summer nights. Strappy, open-toe sandals work with most styles.

• Big, sparkly or jewelled earrings – these are my favourite accessories for dressing up any outfit.

• A long, gold pendant or necklace – wear one instead of earrings, if you prefer.

• A gold cuff or sparkly bracelet – wear one to match either your necklace or your earrings (but not all at the same time).

• Stacks of gold, glittery or jewelled bracelets.

• A giant cocktail ring – for instant glam.

• A white, fake-fur jacket or a sparkly, short bolero are good for covering up on nights out. A smart scarf is also a good evening cover-up option.

Clutch, Jaeger.

Bracelet, Butler & Wilson.

LET'S GET READY TO PARTY

Sometimes we all go over to a mate's to get ready, and so I'll take my make-up and my clothes over there. We'll take turns plugging in our iPods and have a little drink – and a dance – while we get ready. I love the whole atmosphere and preparation of going on a night out, especially with the girls. I usually go and get my hair done at the hairdresser and, depending on where I'm going, I might wear it up or ask my hairdresser Lisa to make it curly, though sometimes I'll just go for a blow-dry. Basically, my advice is, go get your hair done for a night out: I think it's nice just to have time to unwind while you get your hair washed, and I love it when they massage your scalp.

I'll also try and have my nails painted in a really lovely bright colour, like Chanel's Fire. And, for me, a pedicure is a must. Your feet will look gorgeous in high strappy sandals when you've had a pedicure to take any hard skin away. And, of course, I'd make sure that the polish on my hands and feet match.

Make-up-wise, I'd probably dust some bronzer over my face, add a pinch of blusher, and then some lipgloss. I also always carry blotter pads or powder in my bag, as I don't like my face to look shiny – especially in a club, because once I'm up and dancing I won't sit down all night!

skincare

Skincare

How to look after your skin and give your body regular doses of TLC.

I'd love to be one of those people who spends a lot of time on my skin: deep cleansing, massaging and what-have-you every night and day. But, of course, no matter how good my intentions, life just gets in the way.

Like everyone else, though, I want my skin to look nice, but I honestly don't think that it comes down to a regime of complicated daily facial routines. I'm saying this from experience, too, as someone who has suffered from acne. I know that the way our skin behaves is often beyond our control, and that problems are more likely to be down to factors like genes, hormones and nutrition rather than whether we keep up with lengthy skincare rituals. But I also know that, no matter what the reason, not feeling good about your skin can really dent your confidence.

Like the clothes I wear, I think that if I put a little more effort into how I look after myself I will look and feel better – no matter what nature throws my way. Whether it's the brilliantly tingly feeling you get from giving your body an all-over buff in the shower every once in a while, to making sure you get enough fruit and veg in your diet, I know that looking good doesn't come down to some expensive potion from a beauty counter.

So this chapter is all about finding simple ways of helping you look and feel your beautiful best.

The ins and outs of good-looking skin

I know all the mags go on about it, but it really is true that when it comes to having healthy-looking skin, the way you live your life has a big part to play. But that certainly doesn't mean a no-fun, no-party lifestyle – as with everything else, it's all about getting the balance right.

YOU ARE WHAT YOU EAT – AND DRINK

SENSIBLE DRINKING

I don't smoke – it's always been a no-no for me, for obvious reasons, and it also makes your skin age quicker – but I do like to have a drink when I go out with my mates. I won't overdo it, though, and if I think I have, I move on to glasses of water. If you are on a night out, it's a really good idea to drink water in between drinks, as alcohol, like cigarettes, has a drying effect on the skin. **In fact, drinking around one and a half litres of water per day (about eight glasses) is said to do wonders for your complexion – it's like moisturizing skin from the inside. Don't go overboard and drink too much, though, as this can overload your system.**

HEALTHY EATING

When it comes to what you put inside your body, food has a big part to play in having healthy-looking skin. I try to eat a few portions of fruit and veg every day to get all those skin-boosting vitamins in, and, in general, I'll not choose any foods with too much refined sugar or processed fat in them. I have to admit, though, that I do love my crisps, so I will have a bag as a treat every now and again. However, eating too much high-fat, high-sugar stuff can have an adverse effect on your blood system, which could make your skin look pale, spotty and generally not very healthy over time. That doesn't stop me eating natural things like fruit and cheese, which is packed with hair and nail-boosting calcium, as long as I eat it in small quantities.

REGULAR EXERCISE

Think about the lovely rosy look your skin gets you get when you've been walking fast or running for the train, or the way your skin feels an hour after exercising. Having all that blood pumping around your body is great for skin, so get moving around – whether it's a fast walk into town or an aerobics class. It will do something that expensive creams can never do: give you a natural glow.

Exercising will also make you feel more tired at night – and that's a bonus because it means you'll get a good night's sleep. They don't call it 'beauty sleep' for nothing: our skin regenerates itself while we sleep, so it's important to get enough of it. And because I do like a lie-in whenever I get the chance, that's perfectly fine by me!

Try to eat a few portions of fruit and veg every day to get all those skin-boosting vitamins in.

Night and day cream, Stella McCartney.

OK, so now that we've considered the basics of how to make the most of your skin from the inside, let's look at some of the things you can do to make the most of your complexion on the outside.

A little note about skin problems and how to deal with them

I do pay attention to my skin, especially since I had acne in my teens. I was quite lucky in a way because my spots weren't on my skin, they were under it, though I had lots of lumps on my forehead. I had to take really strong medication for it, but because I'm quite a confident person, I never let it get me down. (Although there were times when I thought, 'Please, just go away.')

Most of us get spots at certain points in our lives because they often appear when there are chemical changes in our bodies, but they do tend to disappear over time. If you feel your spots are a bit more stubborn, though, go and see your doctor. It's not being silly or vain, and it could be that medication will make a world of difference. You can also look at the British Association of Dermatologists website for advice (www.bad.org.uk).

When I get spots now I'll maybe use an anti-bacterial face wash for a couple of days. Clearasil Dermalogica do them, and you can get them for sensitive or dry skin, too. I do squeeze spots now and again though I know I shouldn't, as this can spread infection and make my skin worse. The other thing I'll do is drink more water, as it cleans out my system and my skin will benefit too.

Whatever your skin type, here are a few pointers to help you keep your complexion in tip-top condition:

FACIAL CARE

CLEANSE

When it comes to choosing a cleanser, go for one that feels gentle on your face. We all need some natural shine – even if your skin is oily – and anything too harsh will strip natural oils, leaving your skin looking dull. (Think about washing your face with Fairy Liquid and you get the idea!) And that's where cosmetic cleansers come in: they're made without harsh detergents and are kinder to your skin.

Facial wipes

Again, it's a case of trial and error. If you have oily skin, maybe try a gel wash; or if your skin's dry, a cream is probably best. When I'm in a rush I use those 3-in-1 cleansing wipes, but they can be drying, so I wouldn't use them every day.

Make-up remover

If you wear eye make-up, pick up a gentle eye make-up remover. The skin around the eyes is quite delicate, so I'd steer clear of oily ones and instead go for a fresh all-rounder, like Simple Gentle Eye Make-up Remover. I think basic skincare ranges, such as Simple, Boots' own and E45, are all worth trying before splashing out on anything too expensive.

Try: E45 facial skincare, Olay, Johnson's 3-in-1 Facial Cleansing Wipes, L'Oreal, Kiehl's, Clarins Cleansing Duos, Ren, Guinot, Dermalogica and Space.NK.

Many moisturizers now come with in-built sun protection. I'd definitely recommend these.

TONE

I love using toner because it makes your skin feel lovely and fresh after cleansing, and you feel you're really giving your skin a doubly good clean. If you've got oily or normal skin, a simple splash of warm water might do the trick, before patting your face dry with a towel.

Gentle formulas

But, again, regardless of your skin type, if you do like using a toner (and it's not essential, as a good cleanser should do the job), stick with gentle formulas. Even if you've got oily skin, you don't want to apply something with all the harshness of paint-stripper about it. If you've got dry skin, you might want to skip the toner.

Try: Simple, Superdrug Simply Pure, Bliss, Clarins, L'Oreal, Guinot and Space.NK.

MOISTURIZE

I'm always happy to spend a little more on a moisturizer, as it makes all the difference to how your skin feels throughout the day and should keep moisture locked into your skin. Many moisturizers now come with sun-protection, and I'd definitely recommend these; a make-up artist told me that SPFs are a great way of protecting your skin against harsh weather – hot and cold – and that they can have a positive effect on your skin's condition.

When should I change my routine?

My skin type is quite normal – I go through patches where it can be dry, then times when it can be quite oily as well – but I always use different moisturizers for night and day. I used to think it was best to stick to one that I liked for everything, but one make-up artist I worked with suggested it was a good idea to try out different skincare products now and again, as your skin changes all the time. So now I try a variety of products, but I love Guinot, which I buy at my local beauty salon.

CLINIQUE
dramatically different
moisturizing lotion

Guinot have lots of different moisturizers in their range. I'll use a lighter moisturizer for day, a more concentrated one at night, and a rehydrating one if I'm going on a long flight.

Try: Dr Hauschka, Simple, Clinique, Guinot, Nivea, Olay and Stella McCartney Care.

FACIALS

I remember my mum having a face steamer when I was young: it was like a bucket with a bit cut out for your chin to sit on, then you just pushed your head into it. It was quite funny, but it worked. I was complaining about having some blackheads around my nose and my mum said, 'Just put your head into that for a few minutes. That'll get them out.' And it did. So from then on I've always loved steam treatments, and now I go for a facial every four weeks – it really makes a difference.

Facials are a great way of deep-cleansing skin, and I think everyone should treat themselves to one at their local beauty salon if they can, as they are so relaxing and I like the fact that they unclog your pores and get all the grime out. There are treatments suited to your skin type, and all the girls at these places really know what they're doing, so you can get loads of good advice. Do it – your skin will feel so lovely when you come out.

SKIN POLISHING

I try to exfoliate my face every week, as it's a good way of brightening up my skin by removing all the dead skin cells, but I am careful to use one with fine particles in it because they're more gentle and don't dry my skin. You'll find products in Boots and Superdrug as well in the big-brand ranges, such as Clarins and Clinique.

Try: Shiseido Benefiance Pure Retinol Instant Treatment Eye Mask, or SK-II Signs Eye Mask. You can get them at Selfridges, or try Selfridges mail-order if there's not a stockist in your area. Shu Uemura Moisture Eye Zone Mask, from Liberty and Selfridges, is another good treatment. For exfoliation, I like Soap & Glory's Scrub Your Nose In It Exfoliator from Harvey Nichols.

EVERYDAY BODY CARE

I must admit that I tend not to pamper my body as much as my face. I'm particularly bad in winter, because my body's all hidden under layers of clothes and I tend to forget. So now I slather some body lotion on every day – a basic E45 or Nivea lotion is ideal. Doing this really makes a difference. Your skin feels a lot softer, and if you mix a few drops of baby oil in, your skin gets a lovely glow without feeling too greasy. Light body shimmers can be nice, too; apply them around your shoulders and neck when you're wearing a sleeveless top. I like Kiehl's Moisturizer for the body – it's really rich but I think your body can take it, especially during winter.

Try: Nivea Rich Body Moisturizer, E45 Body Lotion, L'Oreal Body Expertise Nutri soft 24hr, Kiehl's Limited Edition Hand & Body Lotion, The Body Shop Body Butter, Soap & Glory Righteous Butter Lite from Harvey Nichols and This Works: Skin Deep Dry Leg Oil.

BODY SCRUBS

I try to exfoliate once a week during my shower to get rid of dry skin. If you do it first thing in the morning it really gets your circulation going. Guinot do a lovely body exfoliator that I use, and I love all the Soap & Glory stuff: they do exfoliators for different parts of your body, including the areas that you forget about, like your elbows. There's nothing worse than seeing white scabby elbows! So now I make sure I scrub mine on a regular basis.

Try: Fake Bake Gin U Wine Body Polish, Origins Ginger Body Smoother, The Body Shop Pink Grapefruit Body Scrub and Liz Earle Energizing Body Scrub.

this works:™
skin
deep
dry
leg oil

Real Skincare Note

I will say that I am good at looking after my feet, and I always go for pedicures when I can as I hate dry skin on my heels and toes. It's also a good idea to have a skin file at home – use it when you can to remove old, dead skin. Follow that up with a good foot cream and your feet should be in tip-top condition.

Try: Exfaxit from Boots, The Body Shop Peppermint Cooling Foot Lotion, Vaseline Intensive Care Healthy Feet & Legs Lotion and E45 Cream.

DE-FUZZING

There's a local beautician called Gemma who regularly comes to my house to wax my legs and bikini line. I used a hair-remover cream to get rid of hairs on my legs, underarms and around my bikini line before I started to wax. It's very rare that I'd shave my legs – maybe on holiday – but in general it makes your hair grow back thicker and coarser. My mate has got a home-waxing kit, but she says she never uses it much as it's quite messy and it's a pain to get out. If you find you don't have time for this, go to a salon, as they usually do the best job.

If you are going on holiday, remember to book in any waxing a couple of days before you leave, as your skin can stay quite red for a while and you don't want to show that off in your new bikini!

Try: Braun Xelle 5180 epilator and Gillette Venus Divine razor; Veet also do a whole range of hair-removal products – take a look at their website, www.veet.co.uk.

PAMPERING

Getting a good massage is just the same as a good facial to me. Every time I go for one, I think, 'why don't I come for these more often?' Also, I tend to drive the car with one arm raised higher up, so one side of my back always seems to be in worse condition than the other. And let's not even start on how much I shouldn't carry in my oversized bag!

But, honestly, massages are amazing for easing out tension and worries, and all the oils they use make your skin feel really pampered. They can be expensive, but not hugely so – and you can choose to focus on a single part of the body: like your back, or just the neck and shoulders. Give yourself a beauty treat and trade one night out for a massage every now and again.

Another treat I love is getting together with my mates for beauty parties. One of them had a baby shower recently and she got in some beauticians to give everyone skincare treats throughout the day. It was so nice – we could have anything from a pedicure to a facial while catching up with each other's news. It was as though her home had turned into *Cutting It* for the day – all we needed was one of those big dryers!

Quite a few of my mates do pamper parties now. So rather than meeting at the pub, we'll go to one of our houses and have a fantastic beautifying session. We might also have a bottle of wine. It's a right laugh. We don't always get beauticians in, but if you want to do that, ask at your local salon if they have an at-home service, or call a local mobile beautician. Search the web, too, as there are some companies who offer a pamper-party services. But for a spur-of-the-moment get-together, just go to Boots or Superdrug and stock up on face packs, nail kits and some really colourful nail polishes. You'll have everything you need for a great girly night in.

hair &
make-up

Hair & Make-up

All you need to know about creating instant looks to suit your style.

I love flicking through the glossies and looking at all the new make-up looks. Even though I don't wear much make-up, I like seeing what make-up artists do on the catwalks every season, and the way that different hair and make-up can totally change the look of an outfit.

We all know, though, that while spending a lot of time getting ready for an event is a real treat, looking good on a day-to-day basis can prove a little more tricky.

But I've discovered that there's no one great secret to how you do your hair and make-up so that you look good; it's more about trying out a few things and picking up tips from mags and your mates.

And I've been really lucky this year to be able to launch my own range of cosmetics, working with the same people, Fragrance and Beauty, who helped me launch my perfume Coleen x last year.

It's been great because, just like the perfume, I've worked with designers at every stage of the development of the cosmetics. I wanted to make sure they really do reflect my personal taste and that they are top quality, while at the same time being something people can afford to have in their handbags. The packaging is a mix of matt and gloss black and my signature is in lilac. I love the range and I hope other people will too.

PREVIOUS PAGE Top, Moschino.

RIGHT Bobbi Brown eyeshadow palettes.

In my job, I chat to lots of make-up artists, and they all agree that their job is not so much about creating big glamorous looks, but about highlighting the features that people feel best about.

And that's what this chapter is basically about: I'm going to focus on how you can put together a basic beauty kit, and give you some practical advice and handy tips to help you make the most of your features.

CONCEALER

I think concealer is a miracle product: dab a little bit onto a blemish and it just seems to disappear. I prefer creamier ones because if your concealer's too dry it can sit in your pores and make your skin look patchy. I use it to even out my skin where it needs it, and I never put a lot on; I've been taught to apply it gently – almost padding it on – with my fingers. Use a concealer brush for a really even cover. (You can get these in Superdrug.) Try: Rimmel Anti-Fatigue Concealer, Yves Saint Laurent Touche Eclat, Laura Mercier Secret Camouflage at Space.NK or Coleen x Photo Light Illuminator.

Tip: try to get a warm colour that matches your skin tone; a concealer that's too light can make your skin look patchy.

TINTED MOISTURIZER

I don't usually wear much make-up during the day, but for evening, or on days when I maybe feel a bit tired, I do use a tinted moisturizer. This gives a nice, sheer coverage that doesn't look too heavy or made-up, and gives my skin a real glow. I like the Guinot one as it seems to be just right for my skin – the shade I use matches my skin colour really well, too. Kiehl's do a good one as well. Try: Boots No.17 Sheer Cover Tinted Moisturiser, Becca Luminous Skin Colour at www.beccacosmetics.co.uk, By Terry Touche Eclat de Teint at Space.NK or Coleen x Tinted Moisturizer. MAC Studio Touch-Up Stick pencil is a really handy concealer for touch-ups on the go.

Powder compact, MAC.

Tip: a little tinted moisturizer goes a long way; it's quite wet, so use just a bit at first and apply it with a foundation brush for even cover. Try to pick one that's got some yellowness in it and that's slightly warmer than your natural skin tone, as this will lift your complexion.

POWDER COMPACT

A powder compact with a mirror is such a handy thing to have in your bag; it's great for touch-ups when you're on the move and, of course, for covering up any shiny bits, which I'm always keen to get rid of. A good powder will even out your skin without drying it out and shouldn't feel too heavy. Try: MAC Microfine Select Sheer powder compact, Chanel Poudre Douce, Bobbi Brown Sheer Finish Pressed Powder or Coleen x Iconic Mineral Powder.

Tip: don't always just choose a translucent shade of powder in the hope that it won't show on top of your skin – choose a warmer shade to match your skin tone for an 'invisible' look. Go to www.bobbi-brown.co.uk and try their colour-match chart.

BRONZER

I often just use a bronzer instead of a blusher, as it gives skin a glow without making it look too rosy. Adding a bit of blusher on the apples of your cheeks is nice for evening. You can also get radiance powders that are pinker and less brown-toned, like Benefit's Dallas Powder Box. Try: Chantecaille Cheek Shade at Space.NK, MAC Bronzer or Coleen x Bronzing Powder.

Tip: Superdrug does a big, fat, bronzer brush for a nice, light sweep: dust the powder on your temples, down the nose, over the tip of the chin and softly on the cheeks. If you have dry skin, try Bobbi Brown's stick bronzer and blend it in gently with your fingertips.

EYESHADOW

If I'm wearing eyeshadow I'll stick with a really neutral colour, like a taupe powder, and apply it just over my eyelids: it's a good idea as it stops your eyes looking too oily and just defines them slightly. Use a blender brush to soften out the powder and stop it from creasing. Try: Nars Eyeshadow duos from Space.NK, MAC Cream Colour Base, Coleen x Eye Shadow Singles and Pop Beauty Eye Class – Smokey Eyes beauty kit at www.popbeauty.co.uk and larger branches of Topshop.

Tip: use a dark eyeshadow instead of eyeliner for a softer look, then blend it in slightly with a blending brush. Lightly dip the brush in water for a more defined line.

EYELINER

Liquid eyeliner and pen styles are too harsh for me, but I occasionally use a soft eye pencil to define my eyes a little. On the rare occasions that I do wear liner, I apply it as close to my eyelash line as possible, but it doesn't matter if the line's not that straight because I always blend it in softly with an eyeshadow brush. Try: Clinique Quick Eyes pencil, Bourjois Kohl & Contour, Dior Crayon Eyeliner, MAC Eye Kohl or Coleen x Precision Eye Definer.

Tip: softer shades, like dark grey or dark brown, are nice and subtle for day. At night, a soft smudge of charcoal liner blended into the outer corner of your eye can add a little evening glamour. The trick with kohl pencil is not to draw it on in a thick, heavy line: apply it lightly and then blend it in with your eyeshadow for a smoky-eye look.

EYEBROW PENCIL

Eyebrows can be really tricky to get right. I've been advised that the best types of brow definer to use are pencils that are soft – almost like eyeshadow – because they give slightly more shape. Gently brush your brows up and out; most eyebrow pencils come with a little brush attached. Always pick a shade as close to your brow colour as possible, and don't go too dark or too light. Try: Rimmel Professional Eyebrow Pencil, No7 Beautiful Brows Pencil or Coleen x Precision Eye Definer.

Tip: if you don't like the idea of using a pencil, apply the tiniest amount of Vaseline to your eyebrows, as this will help to give them shape.

MASCARA

I don't usually wear mascara in the day, but I love brushing some on at night, just to lift my eyes. For me, the best ones are not those that add thickness or length, but the ones that just coat your lashes with a slightly deeper colour than usual. I sometimes get eyelashes applied for special occasions. You can get really natural-looking ones now. Try: Maybelline Great Lash Mascara, Clinique Naturally Glossy Mascara, Chanel Lash Building Mascara, YSL Volume Infini Curl Mascara from Debenhams or Coleen x Magni Lash Mascara.

Tip: try brownish mascara for day, as black can be surprisingly harsh. If you don't like wearing mascara, think about getting your lashes dyed or try using eyelash curlers, as they can make a huge difference.

LIP GLOSS

I never go anywhere without my lip gloss – it's my favourite beauty accessory. I've got loads of colours but my favourites are those that are slightly pinker than my natural lip colour. The great thing about gloss is that you can wear it on its own in the day, and then at night you can wear it on top of lipstick. I'd never lather loads of it on, though, as it can look as if you've got varnish on your lips. Instead I apply a little at a time and top it up throughout the day. I also try to buy good-quality glosses, as cheaper ones can be quite sticky. Try: Lancôme Juicy Tubes, Stila Lip Glaze, MAC Tinted Lipglass, Chanel Glossimer for Lips or Coleen x Wondergloss and Perfect Pout.

Tip: if lip glosses are too shiny for you, try a sheer lip tint: a mixture of lipstick and gloss that gives the lips a soft sheen of colour.

Real Beauty Note

If you want to try out some different looks and learn some top tips about how to apply make-up from the world's top make-up artists, have a look at the following websites. Each has easy-to-follow, step-by-step videos that show you how to do everything from creating smoky eyes to applying different types of foundation. They are a fantastic way to learn the tricks of the trade, and to perfect your own techniques. You don't have to sign up to the websites to get the information and they don't cost anything, so they're well worth a look.

www.beaute-cosmetics.com
www.chanel.com
www.rimmellondon.com
www.lorealparis.co.uk

BRUSHES

A set of make-up brushes is always handy. I've got five brushes in mine: eyeshadow shader, eyeshadow blender, blusher, concealer and a foundation brush for applying tinted moisturizer. You can get great brushes online now. Avoid those that have hairs that fall out easily – it's just so annoying brushing them off your face all the time. Try: MAC, Space.NK and The Body Shop.

Tip: baby shampoo is such a soft detergent that it's ideal for cleaning make up brushes.

Make-up brushes, The Body Shop.

Hair

CUT AND STYLE

Finding the right hairdresser can be a tricky business; I've had everything from quite a cheap haircut to a very expensive one, and I've realized that expensive doesn't necessarily mean better. I think it comes down to who cuts your hair, really. I still use the same local hairdresser, and the girl who cuts mine has been doing it for years. She knows me well, knows what I like and she'll also try different things if I want her to. The thing is, if you feel comfortable with your hairdresser

you'll feel more able to explain the style you want and, more importantly, the one you don't.

WHAT MAKES A GOOD HAIRDRESSER?

A good hairdresser should be able to get a sense of your personal style the minute you walk in the door and be able to gauge how far, or not, you might want to go with a cut. If you're looking for more than a trim, take some pictures along. Your hairdresser should explain what would work for your hair type and what won't, and they may even suggest a gradual change so you don't get a shock if it's not the look you expected.

ABOVE Photograph © Dave Hogan/Getty Images.

WHAT IF I'M NOT HAPPY?

If you're not sure about the way your hair looks when it's finished, don't shy away from telling your hairdresser to have another go at it, just explain what it is you would like them to do – whether it's to take more off or to layer it a bit. My hairdresser says she much prefers it when people say what they think, as she hates the idea of someone walking out feeling upset or unhappy about how they look.

COLOUR

I get the salon colour specialist, who is also my hairdresser, to do my highlights. A good colourist will be totally up-to-date with colour and highlight trends and shouldn't give you anything too out-there or too dated – and highlight trends do seem to date quite quickly.

SHOULD I TRY A DIFFERENT COLOUR?

If you've never had tints or highlights, or if you are thinking about changing your hair colour, your colourist should sit down with you and talk you through the different options, while helping you to find the right shade for your skin tone. I used to have quite a lot of blonde highlights scattered throughout my hair, which was great as it meant they blended in quite well with my natural colour and they didn't need to be constantly re-done. So there's a good tip if you don't want to be in and out of your salon every couple of weeks: ask your colourist to suggest a colour that is low-maintenance and that won't show re-growth too soon.

 Hairclip, Johnny Loves Rosie.

STYLING

I try not to use too many products on my hair – mainly because it is fine and so is easily weighed down by creams and sprays – but I do love using deep-conditioning treatments, like Kérastase, now and again at home, and on holiday especially. You leave them in overnight and they can really improve the condition of your hair after colouring and styling. I also get conditioning treatments at my hairdresser's.

In general, I'd say always go easy on the amount of product you use. I think that no matter what you're using, if you want to avoid looking like you've got Lego-man hair, less is definitely best. Hqhair.com has a fantastic selection of haircare products, with many names that you won't find on the high street, such as Bumble & Bumble and Funky Diva. They do everything from super-smoothers to curl crèmes. Other products I use include Andrew Collinge's Simply No Frizz Salon Shine Glossing Spray – again, it doesn't weigh your hair down. I pick it up at Boots. And, when I do use hairspray, I either stick with the stylists' favourite – L'Oreal Elnette – or James Brown London Hairspray, which I also get at Boots.

Headband, Chanel.

Instant beauty boosters

1 Get a blow dry

If you're going to a 'do', I'd recommend going to the hairdresser, if you can. Getting your hair professionally styled for an event makes you feel amazing; and even if you're not going somewhere special, just booking in for a blow-dry every now and again is a glam treat.

2 Have a mani-pedi

A good manicure and pedicure is something I always treat myself to. Nothing makes you feel smarter than perfectly done hands and feet. Picking your favourite colour gives you an extra lift, too. I like reds in winter and coral shades for summer.

3 Try a body bronzer

Perfect for weddings and parties, or just for an all-round pick-me-up, a spray tan or bronzer application can make all the difference. I'd always go for the lowest level – just a shade darker than your normal skin tone – as that's enough to give your skin a golden glow. You can also do it yourself: try using Vita Liberata Self Tanning Gel (available at Boots). Or try St Tropez and Fake Bake.

PERFUME

It's such a nice finishing touch to spray on a little of your favourite perfume just before you go out. I think we associate so much with scents, especially happy memories. I love it when you smell something that reminds you of being little, for instance, like the smell of flowers in summer, or when you smell a perfume that you recognize, that maybe reminds you of someone or a good time in your life.

CREATING MY OWN SCENT

The French perfumers who helped me create my first perfume, Coleen x, asked me to tell them about the scents that I liked best: from things that I could smell every day to my favourite flowers. Lilies are actually my favourite flowers to look at, but I don't like the way they smell so I couldn't include them! So in the end my perfume was inspired by everything from the aroma of cut grass in summer, to bread fresh out of the oven, and peonies.

Of course, my perfume doesn't actually smell like that, but that's what finding the right scent's all about: you go for one that has something about it that instantly makes you feel good. That's probably why I like to have a choice of perfumes, rather than sticking to the same one, because different ones remind me of different things. In general, though, I prefer fresh, citrusy fragrances. I like Chance Fraise by Chanel because it smells like fresh flowers, and for night, I'll maybe choose a slightly stronger scent, like Flower Bomb by Viktor and Rolf.

My perfume was inspired by the smell of freshly cut grass in summer.

252   Coleen x Eau de Toilette.

HOW TO CHOOSE THE RIGHT SCENT FOR YOU

When choosing a new scent, it's worth bearing in mind that your skin changes throughout the year. Perfume lasts longer in colder weather, so you don't need to spray a lot on. Winter scents tend to be musky and warm anyway, so you only need the tiniest amount. In summer it's a similar thing – our skin produces more oil so perfume tends to stay on for longer. We naturally tend to go for lighter scents in spring and summer, and many of the big-name perfumes now do lighter versions of their big scents. Chloé is now a softer version of the original Seventies blend; while Calvin Klein's Obsession Sheer is a softer scent than the original Obsession, as is Stella McCartney's Stella Sheer .

HOW MUCH SHOULD I SPRAY ON?

Whichever scent I wear, I never put too much on. For me, just a few spritzes after the shower is enough. I don't like perfume to be over-powering, as it can be quite nauseating – for you and anyone who has to sit next to you. In fact, I think one of the nicest ways to get a light scent is by choosing a perfumed body lotion instead of the perfume. The body lotions that match your favourite scents tend to be less intense, but if even they seem too much, you can mix them with some unscented body lotion, which will soften the scent again.

Apart from all the big-name brand perfumes, anyone who loves perfume and is always on the lookout for an individual scent might like to try L'Artisan Parfumeur, Jo Malone, Les Senteurs and Miller Harris – all of which have online boutiques. (See my Real Style File for details.)

Beauty Tip

Perfumes come in different concentrations, from light to intense. Here's a quick guide:

- Eau de cologne: very light. Perfect for mornings.
- Eau de toilette: light. Fine for day.
- Eau de parfum: strong. Best for evenings.
- Parfum: intense. Best used sparingly.

Stella Sheer Eau de Toilette.

Real shopping notes

Before you hit the shops, read my top tips for going shopping.

TAKING CLOTHES BACK

I've become a little less keen to try stuff on in shops now, as changing rooms seem to be getting smaller and busier and the lighting can be a bit iffy, making everything look unappealing. So when I can, I take home the things I've bought and try them on there. Many high-street and designer stores now allow you time to return things that are 'not suitable', which means that if you don't think something looks good on you after all, you can easily take it back and get a refund.

WHEN IS IT OK TO RETURN SOMETHING?

Be warned that shops don't have to give you a refund – it's just their way of giving good customer service – so do ask what the returns policy is before you buy. The only time a store has to give you your money back is if you get home and realize that something you have bought is faulty. If this is the case, take it back straight away: if you leave it too long it's harder to prove that you bought it like that.

HOW MANY DAYS DO I HAVE TO RETURN AN ITEM?

While one shop might just allow you seven days to return something, others will give you up to 28 days, which I think is brilliant service. Again, just remember to find out what the returns policy is before you buy because, although most shops allow you to return clothes, not all will give you a cash refund and they might offer you a credit note to spend in the shop instead.

DO I ALWAYS NEED A RECEIPT?

Whenever you take something back, all shops will ask for the receipt; so keep them safe. I got fed up with losing mine in my purse all the time, so now I keep all my shop receipts together in one place so I know where they are. A friend of mine bought me a great present for my birthday – an Anya Hindmarch purse with 'Coleen's receipts' embossed on the front.

GOOD SERVICE

While I have experienced great service in stores, I've also suffered from people being a bit sniffy – in both smart and not-so-smart places. But the way I see it is that shop staff should always make you feel welcome when you walk into a store. I've worked on a shop floor – and you may have done, too – and whether I worked as an assistant for New Look or Yves Saint Laurent, I would always be polite and helpful and treat people nicely.

Shoes, Faith.

HOW DO I ASK TO SEE THE MANAGER?

If someone makes you feel intimidated when going into a shop, I'd say just don't have a care. People who work in shops are just the same as everybody else – it's their job – so see it for what it is: you are going in to look at things while they are at work. Always ask to speak to the manager if you feel you've been badly treated, though, or call and speak to them when you get home. I think it's always a good idea to be polite when complaining, even if you do feel really annoyed.

IS IT WORTH ASKING THE ASSISTANTS FOR ADVICE?

Of course, sometimes people can be really nice when you don't expect it, and there are plenty of shop assistants who are brilliant at their jobs. I think it's always a good idea to chat to the assistants in fashion stores, as they've probably seen a number of people trying on the same thing as you and know a little more about what works for who.

IS IT OK JUST TO BROWSE TOP DESIGNER STORES?

I'd really recommend that you take time to have a look in designer shops, even if you don't want to buy anything. These are the places where the fashion chain starts, and I think if you are interested in fashion and you love clothes, this is where you can really see how all the big designers put their looks together. Just seeing how the mannequins are dressed can give you some good ideas for styling outfits yourself. But if you are really afraid of going into such shops (which you honestly shouldn't be), go to department stores instead. You'll find top designer collections everywhere, from House of Fraser to Selfridges, and they've usually got nicely planned sections, which are easier to flit in and out of.

PERSONAL SHOPPERS

I'd highly recommend you give personal shopping a go: it's available in most department stores now, and some high-street shops, like Dorothy Perkins and Topshop, also offer style adviser services. And, the brilliant thing is that most stores – whether Harvey Nichols or Topshop – offer personal shopping to customers as a free service, with no obligation to buy. I use the personal shopping service in Harvey Nichols and over the years I have developed a great friendship with the girls there.

HOW CAN A PERSONAL SHOPPER HELP ME?

Whether you are buying casual gear, creating a whole new look, or just getting expert advice on buying a good winter coat, personal shopping is not just about getting kitted out for special occasions; it's a great way to discover new looks and to get some free professional advice. It's just like having your own personal stylist.

HOW WILL THEY KNOW WHAT I'D LIKE?

Your shopper will ask you about the kinds of things you are looking for and then you can both go around the store and pick out some things, or you can just relax and get on with some phone calls and have a coffee while your shopper scours the store for you. A good personal shopper will be bang up-to-date with the latest trends and be able to advise you about the right styles for your shape, as well as suggest clothes that you may never have thought about wearing before.

I never used to take any notice of personal shopper notices in department stores, as I thought this service was for a particular type of customer. Now, though, I use this service whenever I can as I get a lot out of it. Some stores offer the service in bigger branches only, so check out shop websites to see who does what and where. Try it. It's a great thing to do. Just call up and ask for an appointment.

MAKING THE MOST OF THE SALES

Picking up clothes, shoes and accessories in the sales can be a real treat – who doesn't love the idea of getting things half-price? But I'd say try and be careful about spending money on stuff you really might not wear. There's not much point in buying a dress or some new trousers just because they're cheap, so ask yourself if you really love what you're looking at, regardless of whether it's a bargain.

WHAT SHOULD I LOOK OUT FOR?

When I go sale-shopping I tend to stick to looking for classic things that I know I will get wear out of. I think that's what sales are really about: they're a chance to buy good-quality clothes at good prices. If you stick to everyday pieces – like a decent winter coat, plain skirts and sweaters – you can pull them out and wear them year after year. Dressing them up with accessories will easily bring these classic pieces up to date. In fact, I'd say that's a good way of looking at any sale buy: if you stop and have a good think about how it might fit into your own style, with the right shoes and belts, say, you can make a great look out of anything.

WHERE TO LOOK?

The other reason for sticking to plainer things is that many of the high-fashion pieces will have appeared loads in magazines – everyone recognizes them from a particular season, and this can make them date really quickly. Department store sales are some of the best, I think, as you get lots of marked-down designer-wear at good prices. But be quick, as the good stuff usually goes first. Check out the sunglasses section, too – I always pick up some great shades in the sales.

 Shopper, House of Fraser.

SHOPPING ONLINE

The brilliant thing about web shopping is that no matter where you live you can have all the latest styles sent right to your door. From Mango to Marks & Spencer and Missoni, you can buy loads of styles on the net now. There are some great vintage stores to shop at, too. I just love this because, coming from the North, I can't get a lot of the clothes that I have seen and loved in the fashion magazines from anywhere near where I live. So now I regularly use online stores and I've found that not only can you pick up some individual pieces, but when shops are sold out of certain things, you can often pick them up online. A few seasons ago I loved this Warehouse tunic, and I couldn't get it anywhere, then when I logged on to their website, I got one in my size, no problem.

HOW SAFE IS ONLINE SHOPPING?

Net shopping is much more secure and safe than it used to be, and online stores are also usually packed with style tips and advice. The return terms are similar to that of normal shops – usually you can send back anything you don't like and get a refund, although you may have to pay for the return postage. Check the website's terms and conditions before you buy; they should be short and easy to read.

SECRET SALE SHOPS

The other great secret about online stores – designer and high-street – is that most have sale shops the whole year round. You can pick up some great clothes, shoes and accessories at any time, and the discounts tend to be really good – up to 60 per cent off in some cases. And, of course, some things come beautifully wrapped, too, so it's like getting a pressie through the post! (Check out the Real Style File for your guide to the best online stores.)

Top and skirt, DKNY.

DESIGNER BOUTIQUES

It's always worth getting to know people at your local designer boutiques, because then you'll have a better chance of finding something different and possibly picking up a piece that no-one else in your area is likely to have. I love Cricket in Liverpool (which is my local fashion stop), as the girls have a great idea of what I like and they contact me to let me know when new things come in. I spend hours in there just talking and trying clothes on – and having a really enjoyable day. If I'm stuck for something to wear, the girls always come up trumps for me.

TOP UK BOUTIQUES

There are some great designer boutiques outside London now – from Flannels in Manchester, to Cruise in Scotland and Newcastle and, of course, Cricket. If you don't live near any of these places, all these stores have online boutiques, and they all stock different designers or accessories, so they're well worth a look.

Real Style File

Whether you live in Liverpool, Glasgow or Cardiff, you can shop online at every one of the addresses listed here, which means you can track down the styles I've mentioned throughout the book and have them sent straight to your door.

I've split the Real Style File into the same dressing sections as I've covered in the book, making it easier for you to go find specific looks, such as eveningwear or lingerie. I've listed all the familiar brands here, and I've added some other names I thought you might like as well, including a few vintage suggestions.

A tiny amount of the labels I've mentioned in this book don't have online stores, or they only deliver within the US (such as Gap), so I've not listed these. I can't guarantee that you'll be able to find exactly what you're looking for, but you'll discover a whole new list of shops to browse in and styles you're sure to love.

✿ Top, Moschino; skirt, Moschino; shoes, Jimmy Choo.

DRESSES

HIGH-STREET DRESSES
Debenhams: www.debenhams.com
Dorothy Perkins: www.dorothyperkins.com
Freemans: www.freemans.com
House of Fraser: www.houseoffraser.co.uk
La Redoute: www.larcdoute.co.uk
Littlewoods Direct:
   www.littlewoodsdirect.com
Mango: www.mangoshop.com
Miss Selfridge: www.missselfridge.com
Oasis: www.oasis-stores.com
Principles: www.principles.co.uk
Topshop: www.topshop.com
Warehouse: www.warehouse.co.uk

MID-RANGE DRESSES
All Saints: www.allsaintsshop.co.uk
Coast: www.coast-stores.com
French Connection: www.fcuk.com
Karen Millen: www.karenmillen.com
L.K. Bennett: www.lkbennett.com
Manoush, Premium Brands at ASOS:
   www.asos.com
Premium Brands at ASOS: www.asos.com
Reiss: www.reiss.co.uk
Ted Baker: www.tedbaker.com
Urban Outfitters:
   www.urbanoutfitters.co.uk
Whistles: www.whistles.co.uk

DESIGNER DRESSES
Balenciaga at www.matchesfashion.com
Graeme Black at www.brownsfashion.com
Roberto Cavalli at www.net-a-porter.com
Chloé at www.cricketdesignerwear.co.uk
Graham & Spencer at
   www.matchesfashion.com
Issa at www.harrods.com
Lanvin at www.brownsfashion.com
Milly at www.flannelsfashion.com
Moschino Cheap & Chic at
   www.net-a-porter.com
Paul & Joe at www.mywardrobe.com
See by Chloé at www.matchesfashion.com
Tibi at www.net-a-porter.com

VINTAGE DRESSES
Candy Says: www.candysays.co.uk
eBay: www.ebay.co.uk
Martha's Closet:
   www.marthascloset.co.uk
Posh Girl Vintage:
   www.poshgirlvintage.com
Vintage-a-Peel: www.vintage-a-peel.co.uk

JEANS

HIGH-STREET JEANS
ASOS: www.asos.co.uk
Boden: www.boden.co.uk
Dorothy Perkins:
   www.dorothyperkins.com
French Connection: www.fcuk.com
Howies: www.howies.co.uk
Levi's: www.levi.co.uk
Littlewoods Direct:
   www.littlewoodsdirect.com
Mango: www.mangoshop.com
New Look: www.newlook.co.uk

Shoes, Moschino.

Next: www.next.co.uk
Oasis: www.oasis-stores.com
Topshop: www.topshop.com
Uniqlo: www.uniqlo.co.uk
Wrangler at www.littlewoodsdirect.com

MID-RANGE JEANS
Diesel: www.diesel.com
Firetrap at House of Fraser:
    www.houseoffraser.co.uk
Miss Sixty at www.oli.co.uk

DESIGNER JEANS
7 for All Mankind at
    www.johnlewis.com
18th Amendment at
    www.brownsfashion.com
Alexander McQueen at
    www.matchesfashion.com
Balenciaga at www.matchesfashion.com
Chloé at www.net-a-porter.com
Citizens of Humanity at
    www.net-a-porter.com
Hudson at www.ilovejeans.co.uk
J Brand at www.net-a-porter.com
Juicy Couture at www.net-a-porter.com
Radcliffe: www.radcliffedenim.com
Sass & Bide at www.net-a-porter.com
See by Chloé at
    www.matchesfashion.com
Superfine at Matches:
    www.matchesfashion.com
True Religion at
    www.net-a-porter.com
Tummy Tuck at www.ilovejeans.co.uk

VINTAGE JEANS
eBay: www.ebay.co.uk
Rokit: www.rokit.co.uk

TOPS

HIGH-STREET TOPS
Designers at Debenhams:
    www.debenhams.com
George at Asda: www.george.com
House of Fraser: www.houseoffraser.co.uk
La Redoute: www.laredoute.co.uk
M&S Limited Collection:
    www.marksandspencer.com
Principles: www.principles.co.uk
Reiss: www.reiss.co.uk
Topshop: www.topshop.com
Uniqlo: www.uniqlo.co.uk
Urban Outfitters:
    www.urbanoutfitters.co.uk

MID-RANGE TOPS
Antik Batik at Whistles: www.whistles.co.uk
Day Birger et Mikkelson at
    www.flannelsfashion.com
Diesel at www.cruiseclothing.co.uk
Independent Designers: www.asos.com
JJ Park at Oli: www.oli.co.uk
John Smedley: www.johnsmedley.com
Joseph at www.flannelsfashion.com
Michael Stars at www.whistles.co.uk

Paul & Joe Sister, Premium Brands at ASOS:
www.asos.com
PPQ at Oli: www.oli.co.uk
See by Chloé at Urban Outfitters:
www.urbanoutfitters.co.uk
Topshop Unique: www.topshop.com
Twenty8Twelve, Premium Brands at ASOS:
www.asos.com

DESIGNER TOPS
Chloé at www.net-a-porter.com
DKNY at www.harrods.com
Diane von Furstenburg at
www.matchesfashion.com
Marc by Marc Jacobs at
www.net-a-porter.com
Milly at www.harrods.com
Pringle of Scotland at
www.net-a-porter.com
Missoni at
www.cricketdesignerwear.co.uk
Stella McCartney at
www.net-a-porter.com
Tibi at www.flannelsfashion.com

VINTAGE TOPS
eBay: www.eBay.co.uk
Kitty Nation: www.kittynation.com
Martha's Closet:
www.marthascloset.co.uk
Posh Girl Vintage:
www.poshgirlvintage.com

DAYWEAR
HIGH-STREET DAYWEAR
Designers at Debenhams:
www.debenhams.com
Dorothy Perkins: www.dorothyperkins.com

House of Fraser: www.houseoffraser.co.uk
Kurt Geiger Shoes: www.kurtgeiger.com
Mango: www.mangoshop.com
M&S Limited Collection:
www.marksandspencer.com
Miss Selfridge: www.missselfridge.com
Next: www.next.co.uk
Oasis: www.oasis-stores.com
Office shoes: www.office.co.uk
Principles: www.principles.co.uk
Ray-Ban sunglasses at
www.visionexpresssunglasses.com
Topshop: www.topshop.com
Urban Outfitters:
www.urbanoutfitters.co.uk
Warehouse: www.warehouse.co.uk
The White Company:
www.thewhitecompany.com

MID-RANGE DAYWEAR
Coast: www.coast-stores.com
Day Birger et Mikkelsen at
www.matchesfashion.com
French Connection: www.fcuk.com
Hush: www.hush-uk2.com
Karen Millen: www.karenmillen.com
L.K. Bennett: www.lkbennett.com
Premium Brands at ASOS: www.asos.com
Ted Baker: www.tedbaker.com
Toast: www.toast.co.uk
Whistles: www.whistles.co.uk
Uggs: www.uggaustralia.com

DESIGNER DAYWEAR
Burberry: www.burberry.com
Chloé at
www.cricketdesignerfashion.co.uk
D&G Dolce & Gabbana at
www.net-a-porter.com

Top, Chloé; jeans, J Brand.

Freda at www.matchesfashion.com
Matthew Williamson at www.net-a-porter.com
Paul Smith at www.harrods.com
Sonia by Sonia Rykiel at www.brownsfashion.com

VINTAGE DAYWEAR
eBay: www.ebay.co.uk
Martha's Closet: www.marthascloset.co.uk
Posh Girl Vintage: www.poshgirlvintage.com

LINGERIE

HIGH-STREET LINGERIE
Ballet at www.figleaves.com
Best at La Redoute: www.laredoute.co.uk
Chantelle at La Redoute: www.laredoute.co.uk
Fantasie at www.figleaves.com
Freya at www.figleaves.com
Gorgeous at Debenhams: www.debenhams.com
Knickerbox: www.knickerbox.co.uk
La Senza: www.lasenza.co.uk
M&S: www.marksandspencer.com
Odille at Oasis: www.oasis-stores.com
Sloggi at www.figleaves.com
Topshop: www.topshop.com
Triumph at Debenhams: www.debenhams.com
Wonderbra at www.belle-lingerie.co.uk

MID-RANGE LINGERIE
Calvin Klein at www.houseoffraser.co.uk
Elle Macpherson Intimates at www.figleaves.com
La Perla at www.figleaves.com

Princesse Tam-Tam at www.figleaves.com
Rigby & Peller: www.rigbyandpeller.com

DESIGNER LINGERIE
Agent Provocateur: www.agentprovocateur.com
Boudiche: www.boudiche.com
DKNY at www.figleaves.com
Myla: www.myla.com/uk
Stella McCartney Lingerie at www.net-a-porter.com

ACCESSORIES

HIGH-STREET ACCESSORIES
Accessorize: www.monsoon.co.uk
Aldo: www.aldoshoes.com
Argos: www.argos.co.uk
Carvela: www.kurtgeiger.com/carvela
Diva at Miss Selfridge: www.missselfridge.com
Faith: www.faith.co.uk
French Connection: www.fcuk.com
Freedom at Topshop: www.topshop.com
George at Asda: www.george.com
Hobbs: www.hobbs.co.uk
House of Fraser: www.houseoffraser.co.uk
H.Samuel: www.hsamuel.co.uk
Johnny Loves Rosie: www.johnnylovesrosie.co.uk
Kurt Geiger: www.kurtgeiger.com
Mango: www.mangoshop.com
Mikey: www.mikeyjewellery.com
Next: www.next.co.uk
New Look: www.newlook.co.uk
Nine West at the Shoe Studio: www.shoestudio.com
Office shoes: www.office.co.uk

Red Herring at Debenhams:
    www.debenhams.com
Reiss: www.reiss.co.uk
River Island: www.riverisland.com
Rotary at The Watch Hut:
    www.thewatchhut.co.uk
Shellys: www.shellys.co.uk
Swatch:
    www.eu-shop.swatch.com/eshop/uk
Tissot at Goldsmiths:
    www.goldsmiths.co.uk
Topshop: www.topshop.com
Warehouse: www.warehouse.co.uk
Watch Hut: www.thewatchhut.co.uk

MID-RANGE ACCESSORIES
Butler & Wilson:
    www.butlerandwilson.co.uk
Erickson Beamon for Kurt Geiger:
    www.kurtgeiger.com
Karen Millen: www.karenmillen.com

Lola Rose: www.lolarose.co.uk
The Ruby Red Company:
    www.therubyredcompany.co.uk
Sunglass hut: www.sunglasshut.co.uk
Ted Baker: www.tedbaker.com

DESIGNER ACCESSORIES
Burberry: www.burberry.com
Chloé at www.net-a-porter.com
Christian Louboutin at
    www.brownsfashion.com
D&G watches at
    www.thewatchhut.co.uk
DKNY watches at
    www.thewatchhut.co.uk
Erickson Beamon at
    www.net-a-porter.com
Fendi at www.net-a-porter.com
Gucci: www.gucci.com/uk
Jimmy Choo at
    www.cruiseclothing.co.uk
Juicy Couture at
    www.net-a-porter.com
Kenneth Jay Lane
    www.net-a-porter.com
Lara Bohinc at www.harrods.com
Marc Jacobs at www.net-a-porter.com
Mawi at www.brownsfashion.com
Mulberry: www.mulberry.com
Zoe & Morgan at
    www.net-a-porter.com

VINTAGE ACCESSORIES
Barton and Barton:
    www.bartonandbarton.com
eBay: www.ebay.co.uk
Steptoes Dog Vintage Retro
    & Antique Clothing:
    www.steptoesantiques.co.uk

Bag, Freemans.

269

SMART DRESSING

HIGH-STREET SMART

Aldo shoes: www.aldoshoes.com

Designers at Debenhams:
    www.debenhams.com

Dorothy Perkins: www.dorothyperkins.com

Dune shoes: www.dune.co.uk

Freemans: www.freemans.com

George at Asda: www.george.com

House of Fraser: www.houseoffraser.co.uk

Kurt Geiger Shoes: www.kurtgeiger.com

M&S Limited Collection:
    www.marksandspencer.com

Mango: www.mangoshop.com

Miss Selfridge: www.missselfridge.com

Next: www.next.co.uk

New Look: www.newlook.co.uk

Nine West Shoes at www.shoestudio.com

Oasis: www.oasis-stores.com

Office shoes: www.office.co.uk

Principles: www.principles.co.uk

Ray-Bans at
    www.visionexpresssunglasses.com

River Island: www.riverisland.com

Topshop: www.topshop.com

Warehouse: www.warehouse.co.uk

MID-RANGE SMART

All Saints: www.allsaints.co.uk

Black Halo, Premium brands at ASOS:
    www.asos.com

Coast: www.coast-stores.com

French Connection: www.fcuk.com

Jaeger: www.jaeger.co.uk

Karen Millen www.karenmillen.com

L.K. Bennett: www.lkbennett.com

Marlene Birger at www.flannelsfashion.com

Paul & Joe Sister, Premium Brands at ASOS:
    www.asos.com

Reiss: www.reiss.co.uk

See by Chloé at www.net-a-porter.com

Ted Baker: www.tedbaker.com

Twenty8Twelve, Premium Brands at ASOS:
    www.asos.com

Whistles: www.whistles.co.uk

DESIGNER SMART

Alexander McQueen at
    www.brownsfashion.com

Diane von Furstenberg at
    www.matchesfashion.com

Marc by Marc Jacobs at
    www.flannelsfashion.com

Mulberry: www.mulberry.com

Paul & Joe at www.net-a-porter.com

Rag & Bone at www.harrods.com

Sonia by Sonia Rykiel at
    www.brownsfashion.com

Stella McCartney at www.net-a-porter.com

Vanessa Bruno Basics at
    www.brownsfashion.com

SUMMER LOOKS

HIGH-STREET SUMMER LOOKS

American Apparel:
    www.americanapparel.net

Designers at Debenhams:
    www.debenhams.com

Dorothy Perkins: www.dorothyperkins.com

Freemans: www.freemans.com

George at Asda: www.george.com

House of Fraser: www.houseoffraser.co.uk

Johnny Loves Rosie:
    www.johnnylovesrosie.co.uk

Kate Moss at Topshop:
    www.katemosstopshop.com

Mango: www.mangoshop.com

Bracelets, Freedom at Topshop.

Marks & Spencer:
    www.marksandspencer.com
M&S Limited Collection:
    www.marksandspencer.com
Miss Selfridge: www.missselfridge.com
Next: www.next.co.uk
New Look: www.newlook.co.uk
Oasis: www.oasis-stores.com
Principles: www.principles.co.uk
River Island: www.riverisland.com
Topshop: www.topshop.com
Topshop Unique: www.topshop.com
Uniqlo: www.uniqlo.co.uk
Urban Outfitters:
    www.urbanoutfitters.co.uk
Warehouse: www.warehouse.co.uk

MID-RANGE SUMMER LOOKS
Designer jewellery at www.harrods.com
FrostFrench: www.frostfrench.com
Jaeger: www.jaeger.co.uk
Joseph at www.flannelsfashion.com
Paul & Joe Sister, Premium Designers at
    ASOS: www.asos.com

Reiss: www.reiss.co.uk
See by Chloé at Premium Designers at
    ASOS: www.asos.com
Ted Baker: www.tedbaker.com

DESIGNER SUMMER LOOKS
3.1 Phillip Lim at
    www.matchesfashion.com
DKNY at www.net-a-porter.com
Dries van Noten at
    www.brownsfashion.com
Milly at www.flannelsfashion.com
Moschino Cheap & Chic at
    www.net-a-porter.com
Sportmax at
    www.matchesfashion.com
Stella McCartney at
    www.net-a-porter.com

VINTAGE SUMMER LOOKS
Candy Says: www.candysays.co.uk
eBay: www.ebay.co.uk
Posh Girl Vintage:
    www.poshgirlvintage.com

Blouse, vintage; corsage,
Johnny Loves Rosie.

271

GYMWEAR

HIGH-STREET GYM LOOKS

American Apparel:
   www.americanapparel.net
Deha at www.sweatybetty.com
Figleaves: www.figleaves.com
Littlewoods: www.littlewoods.com
Nike: www.Nike.com
Reebok: www.reebokstore.co.uk
Run and Become:
   www.runandbecome.com
Sheactive: www.sheactive.co.uk
Sweaty Betty: www.sweatybetty.com
USA Pro at www.sheactive.co.uk

DESIGNER GYM LOOKS

Gucci: www.gucci.com/uk
Stella McCartney for Adidas:
   www.adidas.com

TRAVEL WARDROBE

HIGH-STREET TRAVEL LOOKS

Accessorize: www.monsoon.co.uk
Bravissimo: www.bravissimo.com
Butterfly by Matthew Williamson at
   Debenhams: www.debenhams.com
Dorothy Perkins: www.dorothyperkins.com
Figleaves: www.figleaves.com
Freemans: www.freemans.com
French Connection: www.fcuk.com
Freya at www.figleaves.com
George at Asda: www.george.com
Holiday Shop at www.asos.com
Kate Moss for Topshop:
   www.katemosstopshop.com
Kurt Geiger Shoes: www.kurtgeiger.com
La Redoute: www.laredoute.co.uk
Mandarina Duck luggage at John Lewis:
   www.johnlewis.com
Mango: www.mangoshop.com
M&S Limited Collection:
   www.marksandspencer.com
Mikey: www.mikeyjewellery.com
Miss Selfridge: www.missselfridge.com
Monet at www.debenhams.com
Next: www.next.co.uk
Nine West at www.shoestudio.com
Oasis Holiday shop: www.oasis-stores.com
Office shoes: www.office.co.uk
Pamela Mann Tights: www.tightsplease.com
Panache at www.bravissimo.com
Radley luggage at House of Fraser:
   www.houseoffraser.co.uk
Topshop: www.topshop.com
Tripp luggage at Debenhams:
   www.debenhams.com
Vitamin A at www.figleaves.com
Warehouse: www.warehouse.co.uk

Top, Republic.

MID-RANGE TRAVEL LOOKS
Joseph at www.flannelsfashion.com
Reiss: www.reiss.com
Twenty8Twelve, Premium Designers at
    ASOS: www.asos.com
Whistles: www.whistles.co.uk

DESIGNER TRAVEL LOOKS
3.1 Phillip Lim at
    www.matchesfashion.com
Biba at www.matchesfashion.com
Chloé at
    www.cricketdesignerwear.co.uk
Emilio Pucci at www.net-a-porter.com
Juicy Couture at www.net-a-porter.com
Melissa Odabash at www.odabash.com
Milly at www.net-a-porter.com
Missoni at
    www.cricketdesignerwear.co.uk
Paul & Joe at www.net-a-porter.com
Roberto Cavalli at
    www.flannelsfashion.com
Wright and Teague jewellery:
    www.wrightandteague.com
Zoe & Morgan at www.net-a-porter.com

TRAVEL BEAUTY
Dove Summer Glow at www.superdrug.com
Fake Bake at www.salonlines.co.uk
Johnson's Holiday Skin: www.boots.com
Piz Buin 1: www.boots.com St Tropez at HQ
    hair: www.HQhair.com
Sisley Body Sun Cream SPF 15:
    www.harrods.com; www.johnlewis.com
This Works: www.thisworks.com

WINTER

HIGH-STREET WINTER LOOKS
Designers at Debenhams:
    www.debenhams.com
Dorothy Perkins: www.dorothyperkins.com
French Connection: www.fcuk.com
George at Asda: www.george.com
House of Fraser: www.houseoffraser.co.uk
Kate Moss at Topshop:
    www.katemosstopshop.com
Mango: www.mangoshop.com
Marks & Spencer:
    www.marksandspencer.com
M&S Limited Collection:
    www.marksandspencer.com
Miss Selfridge: www.missselfridge.com
New Look: www.newlook.co.uk
Next: www.next.co.uk

❀ Sandals, Gap.
❀ Travel kit, This Works.

Oasis: www.oasis-stores.com
Principles: www.principles.co.uk
River Island: www.riverisland.com
Topshop: www.topshop.com
Topshop Unique: www.topshop.com
Uniqlo: www.uniqlo.co.uk
Urban Outfitters:
    www.urbanoutfitters.co.uk
Warehouse: www.warehouse.co.uk

MID-RANGE WINTER LOOKS

All Saints: www.allsaintsshop.co.uk
FrostFrench: www.frostfrench.com
Hoss Intropia at www.net-a-porter.com
Jaeger: www.jaeger.co.uk
Karen Millen: www.karenmillen.com
L.K. Bennett: www.lkbennett.com
Radcliffe, Premium Brands at ASOS:
    www.asos.com
Reiss: www.reiss.co.uk
See by Chloé at www.net-a-porter.com
Ted Baker: www.tedbaker.com
Twenty8Twelve, Premium Brands at ASOS:
    www.asos.com
Uggs: www.uggaustralia.com
Whistles: www.whistles.co.uk

DESIGNER WINTER LOOKS

3.1 Phillip Lim at
    www.matchesfashion.com
Aquascutum at www.brownsfashion.com
Burberry at www.net-a-porter.com
DKNY at www.net-a-porter.com
Freda at www.matchesfashion.com
Marc Jacobs at www.matchesfashion.com
McQ by Alexander McQueen, Premium
    Brands at ASOS: www.asos.com
RM by Roland Mouret at
    www.net-a-porter.com

VINTAGE WINTER LOOKS

eBay: www.ebay.co.uk
Rokit: www.rokit.co.uk
Vintage a Peel: www.vintage-a-peel.co.uk

EVENING

HIGH-STREET EVENINGWEAR

Designers at Debenhams:
    www.debenhams.com
Faith: www.faith.co.uk
French Connection: www.fcuk.com
House of Fraser: www.houseoffraser.co.uk
Kate Moss Topshop:
    www.katemosstopshop.com
M&S Limited Collection:
    www.marksandspencer.com
Miss Selfridge: www.missselfridge.com
Monsoon: www.monsoon.co.uk
Next: www.next.co.uk
Oasis: www.oasis-stores.com
Osman Yousefzada at Mango:
    www.mangoshop.com
Principles: www.principles.co.uk
Topshop: www.topshop.com
Urban Outfitters:
    www.urbanoutfitters.co.uk
Wallis: www.wallisfashion.com

274   ❀ Dress, Stella McCartney.

❀ Earrings, Erickson Beamon
    at Debenhams.

MID-RANGE EVENINGWEAR
Jaeger: www.jaeger.co.uk
Karen Millen: www.karenmillen.com
L.K. Bennett: www.lkbennett.com
Manoush at www.net-a-porter.com
Ted Baker: www.tedbaker.com
Wheels & Doll Baby, Premium brands at
    ASOS: www.asos.com
Whistles: www.whistles.co.uk

DESIGNER EVENNGWEAR
3.1 Phillip Lim at
    www.matchesfashion.com
Amanda Wakeley:
    www.amandawakeley.com
Burberry: www.burberry.com
Calvin Klein at www.net-a-porter.com
Chloé at www.cricketdesignerfashion.co.uk
D&G Dolce & Gabbana at www.net-a-
    porter.com
Dolce & Gabbana at
    www.flannelsfashion.com
Freda at www.matchesfashion.com
Jimmy Choo at www.net-a-porter.com
Lanvin at www.cricket designerwear.co.uk
Matthew Williamson at
    www.net-a-porter.com

Paul Smith at www.harrods.com
Sergio Rossi at www.net-a-porter.com
Sonia by Sonia Rykiel at
    www.brownsfashion.com
Temperley London at www.cricket design-
    erwear.co.uk
YSL at www.brownsfashion.com

VINTAGE EVENINGWEAR
eBay: www.ebay.co.uk
Martha's Closet: www.marthascloset.co.uk
Posh Girl Vintage:
    www.poshgirlvintage.com

SKINCARE
Bliss: www.blisslondon.co.uk
The Body Shop: www.thebodyshop.co.uk
Braun at Argos: www.argos.co.uk
Clarins at Debenahms:
    www.debenhams.com
Clinique at Debenahms:
    www.debenhams.com
Dr Hauschka www.drhauschka.co.uk
E45 facial skincare at Boots:
    www.boots.com
Efasit: www.boots.com
Elemis Rehydrating Rose Petal Cleanser:
    www.debenhams.com

✿ Shoe, Jimmy Choo.

Fake Bake at www.salonlines.co.uk
Gillette at Superdrug: www.superdrug.com
Guinot: www.simplyproducts.co.uk
Johnson's at Boots: www.boots.com
Kiehl's at Space.NK: www.spacenk.co.uk
Liz Earle: www.lizearle.com
L'Oreal at Superdug: www.superdrug.com
Nivea at Boots: www.boots.com
Olay at Asda: www.asda.com
Origins: www.origins.co.uk
Ren: www.renskincare.com
Space.NK: www.spacenk.co.uk
Shiseido at Harrods: www.harrods.com
Simple at Superdrug: www.superdrug.com
Sisley Botanical Fluid Moisturiser:
    www.harrods.com; www.johnlewis.com
SK-II at Harrods: www.harrods.com
Superdrug Simply Pure:
    www.superdrug.com
Vaseline Intensive Care at Boots:
    www.boots.com
Veet: www.veet.co.uk
YSL Cleansing Silky Balm Radiance
    Revealer: www.debenhams.com

HAIR & MAKE-UP

Andrew Collinge: www.boots.com
Becca: www.beccacosmetics.co.uk
Benefit: www.benefitcosmetics.co.uk
Bobbi Brown: www.bobbibrown.co.uk
Boots No7: www.boots.com
Boots No.17: www.boots.com
Bourjois: www.boots.com
By Terry at Space.NK: www.spacenk.co.uk
Chantecaille at Space.NK:
    www.spacenk.co.uk
Clinique at Debenhams:
    www.debenhams.com

Dior make-up at Debenhams:
    www.debenhams.com
James Brown London: www.boots.com
Lancôme at Debenhams:
    www.debenhams.com
Lanvin Rumeur: www.johnlewis.com
L'Artisan Parfumeur:
    www.laboutiquedelartisanparfumeur.com
Les Senteurs: www.lessenteurs.com
L'Oreal Elnette: www.boots.com
Laura Mercier at Space.NK:
    www.spacenk.co.uk
Jo Malone: www.jomalone.co.uk
MAC: www.maccosmetics.co.uk
Maybelline at Superdrug:
    www.superdrug.com
Miller Harris: www.millerharris.com
Nars at Space.NK: www.spacenk.co.uk
Pop Eye Class: www.popbeauty.co.uk
Oil of Olay at Boots: www.boots.com
Rimmel at Superdrug: www.superdrug.com
Stila cosmetics: www.hqhair.com
Vita Liberata: www.vitaliberata.com
Yves Saint Laurent at Debenhams:
    www.debenhams.com

Powder compact, MAC.

ACKNOWLEDGEMENTS

With thanks to:

Paul Stretford, my business manager and agent; Rachael Hassall, my PA; Jane Aspinall, my Project Coordinator at Proactive Talent management; Ian Monk, my publicist; Sally Annett and all her team at Harper Collins; Caragh McKay; David Venni; Brendan Robertson and Jackie Dixon. Thank you all for making this project happen. Without all of you I doubt this project would have gone much further than the ideas stage. And a big thank you to Harvey Nicholls, Manchester and Cricket, Liverpool for loaning so many of your gorgeous clothes to us. I am indebted to you all and thank you for your time, patience and dedication.

HCR

 Top, vintage.

 ENDPAPERS Dress, Temperley London; shoes, Jimmy Choo.